They Want My Soul

They Want My Soul

Patricia Charles

authorHOUSE®

AuthorHouse™
1663 Liberty Drive
Bloomington, IN 47403
www.authorhouse.com
Phone: 1-800-839-8640

First published by AuthorHouse   08/05/2011

ISBN: 978-1-4567-6913-0 (sc)
ISBN: 978-1-4567-6912-3 (ebk)

Library of Congress Control Number: 2011906942

Printed in the United States of America

Any people depicted in stock imagery provided by Thinkstock are models, and such images are being used for illustrative purposes only.
Certain stock imagery © Thinkstock.

This book is printed on acid-free paper.

CONTENTS

DEDICATION

This book is dedicated to my two children Jason Richard Charles (who lives in Trinidad), and Janelle Safia Atwell (who currently resides in Philadelphia), both of whom I love dearly, and am immensely proud of. I thank you for choosing me to have your earthly experiences through and with. I know we had many challenges but the Lord continues to bring us through them all.

Know that you can do All things through Christ who strengthens each and every one of us. This race we are running is neither for the strongest, nor the swiftest but for those who can endure to the end. And remember in all that you do put God first!

ACKNOWLEDGEMENTS

I am pleased to express my sincere gratitude to many of the faculty and administration at Lehman College, where the guidance and further courses I received prepared me to write this book. Particularly Professor Argeros, my Sociology Professor.

I also want to acknowledge the following individuals who, in various ways to one degree or another, they have either encouraged me, assisted and stood by me during my journey, Deacon Elizabeth Gadson, Laurel Barrette, Beverly Robinson, Claudette Burke, Etta Effatt, Estelle Vaughn, Hazel Gaffford, Dorothy Johnson and Shirley Christian, ... Thank you all.

To three special friends who were very instrumental in this journey, Cheryl Anthony, Monica Baptiste and Cheryl Logan. Your genuine friendship shows that the human heart can unite us and cause us to care for each other.

And, to all my employers; you were the passage way for me to go through the sea on dry ground to where God wanted me to be today. Great is the Lord!

I thank Dr. Paul from North Carolina, who has been a spiritual guide over the years, but especially through the writing of this book. I had to draw on Dr. Paul's spiritual advice and biblical knowledge on many occasions to help me complete this book.

A special thanks to my church families at Church of the Abiding Presence and Gethsemane Baptist Church for allowing God's word to be preached without any form of compromise.

INTRODUCTION

Since 2007, the word 'economic' has been a buzz word in the print and visual media. We hear of economic crises, economic collapse, economic hard times, economic stimulus, economic recession, economic meltdown, and the word lives on. Oh! Did I mention economic distress and economic dislocation? This is the net of pain in which ordinary people find themselves. While media looks at the economic situation in terms of percentages of the labor market and GNP's, the ordinary people want to talk about the reality of individual hardships, sacrifices, and loss of the foundation they once had for the years to come. People have to live with the reality of losing the bread, the butter, and the tables around which to have a piece of bread and butter, along with the shelter over their head, where they can eat, sleep, and be a family. I can't imagine this would ever happen, but I mention it anyway. What if peoples' lives don't improve or return to some normalcy soon? The government may have to legislate removing belts from the millions of unemployed as a suicide prevention law.

Since this book would attempt to inform readers on peoples fight for their soul in today's economy, it puts the spotlight on me. I would present my own personal experience as a black immigrant woman and my years of working in the homes of two of my white employers who wanted to take my soul while in their employ.

In a few short years of living in America, my life would go from living comfortably away from God to one of being in God's purpose. My life would have its share of good times, where I enjoyed making money and spending it in social and fashionable circles. The good times were the parties, the boat rides, the bus rides, the excessive shopping and spending, a carefree indulging in the glitz and glamour of the world.

Having been raised in the Catholic Church in Trinidad, there was very little time for going to church in America. I made myself believe that. Yet, I was always aware and mindful of the spiritual aspect of my life. I knew life had to be more than just work, or having a good time and occasionally attending a Church on Sundays. Some days, this question would inhabit my thoughts: Am I a spiritual being having a physical experience or vice versa? And which of these two natures should I feed and satisfy? Hours later, I would manage to repel those thoughts without a decisive response.

When I worked for my employers, I had to suppress and quench the spiritual aspect of who I am. The environments in which Childcare Providers work seldom facilitate Christian expression. There were so many things I had to accept that were contrary to my Christian beliefs. Then, for me the source of life was the weekly salary I made, although it was not commensurate with my experience and academic skills. Christian faith and dogma did not have much of an influence in my life.

Looking back on my entire journey, I knew God had a plan for my life all along. But God allowed me to try it my way and the world way. God allowed me to come to the end of myself and, to turn to His way and His plans for my life. A day would come when I would readily respond again to God's calling. And God would now take my life another way, His way.

I worked as a Childcare Provider for over fifteen years and did enjoy working with children and still do. Work is good and work should be enjoyable. We should look forward to going to work, when it serves to enhance meaning in our day to day lives. The objective for going to work should not simply be to earn money. When getting pay for working was chiefly what work meant to me, I knew God was calling me to reconsider my calling, my purpose for being. I made a decision to end my employment with Sarah, after thirteen years.

Not long after, as God was moving in a new direction in finding true purpose for my life, God allowed me to go through a brief time of providing Childcare for Daniel and his wife. It was there that God would open my eyes to deep seated racism in the mindset of this family, and God did so to let me see that, once and for all, I had to leave Childcare work, if I wanted to find true purpose in life. I have set aside two chapters in this book to recount the experiences with Sarah and Daniel, all of which God was preparing for me to step out on faith to a new life in Christ.

God did not make things come easy for me. I think God wanted to see if I would remain focused this time and trust Him and not return to the dead end work of Childcare. Being unemployed and as I looked for employment of any kind, I found the country experiencing a recession. No one was responding to the resumes and application I was submitting. I came to realize that this was the time I had to spend with God to yield to my calling.

As I took time to reflect on my current unemployment, I soon discovered the purpose God had for me. It was connected to the work I was doing, because racism in the field of Childcare was muddling my sense of being in God's purpose. When I heard the very still small voice of the Holy Spirit whispering "This is what I called you to do," my faith leaped a hundred miles ahead of my body. What a revelation! I would run. No longer could fear, materialism, and complacency accompanied by racism encapsulate my existence from finding and pursuing purpose in God.

This book is the voice of an ordinary African American woman, my story, my dreams, my reality and my unequivocal faith in God and his purpose for my life. It tells the story of my dreams that were being shattered one by one, yet I still refuse not to dream. I didn't give up because I had to trust God and try to understand what gave rise to where I had found myself. What kept my dreams alive, were my courage, confidence, and convictions in my God who gave me the dreams. Now God is remaking those dreams in HDV-High Definition Vision. In my view, people who now find themselves on the side streets of economic loss should not focus entirely on this economy and on themselves alone to reach the high way of economic prosperity and aspirations in America. They need to look elsewhere, back to the source of their very being and existence, to God who is not only the giver of life, but also the guardian of our soul.

As I present my personal experience in the book I would share my thoughts on what role the church is playing in the lives of its adherents. I must ask is the Church a source of relief to the captives or a Force of Further Grief to those who are already grieving. Centuries ago, when the Church did have influence on the state (the reader may refer to the times of Constantine and Justinian), and when the Church truly exemplified the law of love in early Christendom, the church was far more effective. Again I must ask: is the 21st century Christian Church out of the way of Christ?

In the last chapter of this book, I would mention some things I have learned on this journey. All that I have learned is bound to the understanding that, I no longer look to nor do I set my mind on climbing the steps of success and easy living. I found the way to having staying power. For, if those who tried to take my soul failed, now I am convinced that I have the answer for anyone who would find themselves where I was, a minute before midnight of a crushed broken character. I am still standing with the radiance of my soul intact.

I proudly present my story.

I

THE JOURNEY BEGINS

One day I woke up and I found myself fired and unemployed. A few weeks later, I applied for unemployment benefits and was denied. While many people who became unemployed were fortunate to be in line to receive ninety nine weeks of unemployment assistance, I was put out of the line. It is because one of my former employers' blocked the approval of my unemployment benefit. I was beginning to drift into a dark place. I found myself having to ask some hard and soul searching questions "How did I end up here?" "How did I find myself in this situation?" "What led me to be in this dry place?" "Should I blame myself for being out of work?" Then too, for the first time I found myself trying to understand how did America, the world's economic engine, find itself deep in the throes of a world recession? And somewhere deep beneath the rubble of questions, there loomed a spiritual question: Was my employer trying to take my soul?

This was the right time for me to take a look back at my own situation in order to understand the path I entered into alone as a woman and as an immigrant in this society.

Where am I to go from here to find the truth for where I am to in the future? If I am to find truth, I have had to apply myself reflectively and through learning to arrive at the truth.

In coming to America, I was introduced to the Childcare Profession soon after my arrival. I came with a solid educational background. I had a good history of employment. Being given the offer for immediate employment, I took it. Not wanting to wait on employment in my field of learning and past experience,(because of my residential status) I went into the Childcare profession. I was a single parent and the Childcare profession was, and still is, a readymade profession for many immigrants. The profession requires a new pool of immigrant workers to replenish its working force of low paying jobs. No one ever sat me down and shared the real scenario of the reality of this profession, and the difficulty to exit and transition into other professions, until I was neck deep in it. By then I realized I was completely misled. I was trapped in a work that employers did not value your humanity and worth. I had planned to work in the field for a little while and then go back to college to get a degree in a profession that will give me the stability, the security and the benefits that such an educational investment guarantees.

I migrated to this country about 20years ago and about three years later my son Jason and my daughter Janelle came to live with me. Jason, however after spending about a year returned to Trinidad. Living in America was quite a cultural shift. As such, like so many immigrants who came before me, I was wrestling with my decision to migrate; I too wondered: Did I make the right decision? Was it in vain? Who really benefitted from this migration? Would I find a better future here?

Most immigrants come to this country to "do better" and I was no exception. I came with my own set of Administrative and Accounting Skills, but without a green card. Without it, I was told I could not enter the workforce. The first three years I lived here I did sleep-in jobs. Those early days were materially difficult and spiritually troubling. I had left my children with my mother and here I was taking care of someone else's children. I had left a comfortable home and here I was sleeping in someone else's home. I came with hopes and dreams of one day having my children with me and of continuing the pursuit of my academic degree, like all immigrants the journey is for the American dream of homeownership and a "good" job. I knew I had to get my residency first in order to accomplish those hopes and dreams.

When I left Trinidad, I had completed the first year of a degree program at The University of the West Indies. I never forgot that education was always the key for success. The charge of many Trinis, as we are called, comes from the influence of our first and late Prime Minister, Dr. Eric Eustace Williams. He always reminded us that our future and any nation's future were in the book bags of the children, and so education was of great importance to me. Dr. Williams' interaction with us shaped my sense of learning, and knowing that once you have an education, it cannot be taken away from you.

When I told my mother to send Jason and Janelle up one summer, it was indeed a nerve wrecking period in my life. I was very nervous about this decision, even though I am normally a calm, cool and collected individual. For the first time in my life I would be totally responsible for my children without any outside support either from family or social support systems. In our family we all took care of each other's children. At any given time everyone of the aunts, uncles, grandmothers, in-laws, cousins were all so willing and simultaneously ready to contribute to the welfare and raising up of one another's children. With a large network of family, I had an excellent support system for Jason and Janelle in Trinidad. Yes in my case it took a village to literally and figuratively raise my two children and it was a wonderful experience. I would do it all over again. Everyone knew my children and everyone looked out for them. Even correcting them if need be.

Now, fast forward to America, Staten Island, where there were no family members present. I was a nervous wreck. I had a good friend there-Cheryl Anthony—who helped me and we are still friends even today. At the time I questioned my own abilities as a parent to take on parenting two children on my own. I knew at that point I could no longer do live-in jobs and had to get a job as a Childcare Provider, where I could travel back and forth. I found one of the lower eastside but that did not last too long because the family moved away. That is one of the negative factors with this type of work. Employers move away at a moment's notice and you are without a job. These employers do not consider the humanity of Childcare workers that we too have a life to live.

Not too long after I went to work with Sarah. I started this job in April 1994 and stayed until July 2007 at which point I tendered my resignation. I was not too sure about the length of time I was going to be with this family but we obviously were a good fit together for me to have spent thirteen years with them. This was the best working situation in comparison to the others. However, there were no health benefits or health insurance with the job. I remember having fibroids removed and Mrs. S did pay me for all the weeks I was at home and for that I was very grateful.

As Childcare Providers we do bring a lot to the profession. Although it is looked upon without much appreciation or as a job for which not much importance is given to it, this job takes a lot out of you as a person. Having to deal with cranky and colicky babies from 8a.m to 6:30pm does wear on a person. A Childcare Provider often deal with troublesome, rude and disrespectful children on a daily basis, whose parents would rather that someone else deal with those challenges. It takes a special kind of person to wake up every day and go to these jobs not knowing what to expect from some of these children from one day to the next, and without much support and co-operation from the parents.

When I came to this country, I came having a strong sense of self and identity—(A healthy self-esteem). However, over time it became clear to me that as an immigrant I should not have been so comfortable with who I am. I was even cautioned about my proper diction from one of my step-sisters who said I spoke "too proper". That was the way I was taught to speak and I was not going to change that about myself. I was more than the job. I brought some other skills which were unique to me. Our island is a cosmopolitan paradise where people of various ethnicities and religions live peacefully and as our anthem states it best: "where every creed and race finds an equal place". As a result of this exposure to other ethnic groups, I was capable of associating associating and getting along with people of various backgrounds. Also as a born and raised Catholic, I was always mindful that we are all created equal in the eyes of the creator.

I am sure that many immigrants have provided childcare for children who have become doctors, lawyers, mayors and leading citizens in this country. I find it interesting that the immigrant childcare workers, who are caring shepherds of some of these challenging children seldom, receive any recognition for their work as mothers, teachers, nurses, social workers, athletic coaches and hairdressers. We are even expected to role play with these children thus giving them their first lessons in theatre and drama.

How many of you knew this about Childcare work? If I did not have a good moral, spiritual and sense of self worth, I could easily have relinquished my soul, my future, to my former employers. These employers would want to control your existence and journey in this life. For a Childcare Provider hopes and dreams does not matter to the employers and you dare not reveal or share them with your employers. That could be grounds to get fired.

My journey continues on . . .

II

HOPES AND DREAMS

I heard that America is a land of hopes dreams and opportunities. It was all that was important to me. I had big hopes. I had endless dreams and I would wait for an opportunity. I have also heard that the Aquarians live their lives trying to save the world and always trying to make the world a better place. But I was missing what really mattered: the vision God gives for our life's journey.

The mistake most of us make is that we try to single handedly accomplish these dreams on our own. As long as we have a job, a car, money on hand, these are the hopes and dreams we pin our future hopes and dreams on. We tend to reach for a more prosperous future based on the workers creed: "work harder." This is where most people focus most of their hopes dreams and sense of security. By so doing, they tend to disregard the other aspects of what drive lives to meaning, a connection to God. We all know that being able to work is good. The fruits of our labor enable us to gain some degree of an independent life; it gives meaning and satisfaction to our self worth.

But work can also be a tool used by employers to limit a worker's hopes and dreams, as I would soon find out. Most employers have a psychological advantage, over workers, because workers tend to build their hopes and aspirations upon their work. "Are employers greater or better people than you? Isn't it by their privilege and opportunities, and sometimes by much wrongdoing, they are where they are? Employers are not members of the pantheon of gods or Pharaohs as some may want to appear to workers. They lord themselves over their workers. This is why workers need more than work to give meaning to life. Because, when all hope seems to have faded away, when dreams are not realized, and when employers try to take away the lifeline of work from people who spent years at working hard, the employer does not even look back at you to see where you have fallen. I have learned this firsthand: if you are going to fall, be sure to fall on your knees. From this posture you'll always have a true future and a hope. For this is when God shows up. He is always nearby, a reliable companion. So I have come to realize, not a minute too late, that I must always put God first in my life.

As I look around I cannot help but wonder why God's people are just going around in the same circles, re-infecting each other with their lack of purpose, lack of vision, and lack of true mission. The Bible tells us that without a vision the people perish; without your personal vision you will perish. The Bible also tells us to write this vision, though it tarries, it will come to pass (Habakkuk 2:1-5). The script has been written in our heart. It was given to us to bring into existence, things not yet seen on this earthly journey. You have to be persistent in pursuing what God placed in your heart. I am in complete agreement with John Henry

Newman who once said: "We have all been made for a definite purpose."

Although you are getting older, don't give up the vision. The older years offer clearer vision of God and purpose for being. It is all the more reason you should not die with a life of failed hopes and broken dreams. Instead we must find the path to a life inspired by a vision of divine calling and live by it. This life offers peace in every area of life's turbulence. Even people who may have been prepared for these tough economic times have discovered that their preparation was not good enough. Didn't they work hard to find happiness? Or maybe they still did not work hard enough?

In fiercely protecting my soul, I have had enough of life's lessons and experiences to know that whatever purpose God places in your heart, He will see it to completion. I have learned that to continue to seek Him and make myself available to God otherwise I may not have seen the purpose here today to tell my story. I have had to keep looking at God's vision for my life and my journey. I have had to keep guard of my soul, even as I have had to labor to maintain myself worth. There are many vision killers around us who are always trying to kill the vision God gave to us for a better future. I had to guard my vision at all costs, waiting for the day when it will come to pass. Even without a job and any source of income. I have not fallen, because from my knees I always rise again.

It is never easy to keep focus on God's plan for our lives. Why? It is simply because we have so many choices in our day to day life. But as Thomas Morton once said: "When we are faced with an easy choice and a hard choice, the hard choice is the way of God." For a time, I looked everywhere and to everyone, looking for what God had shown me to do. I wanted easy and safe choices, if someone could offer it to me. I searched high and I searched low, expecting someone to give me a word which would lead me into finding my purpose. But there was no one in my every day encounters who themselves were in their place of purposeful living. I was wrestling with my own sense of purpose. Not until I took God at His word, that "in Him I live, and move, and have my being", that I focused my journey on completing the purpose of God for my life. It was about that time some people may have begun wondering about me. I could no longer relate to those around me as I had done in former times. They began to see my transformation. God was doing a new thing with me. So that being without a job, I was still able to see God's purpose before me. God was revealing His purpose for my life, and I was beginning to understand it all. To my reader I say: Few other times in your life you would find as resplendent as when God begins to sharpen your vision on what your purpose in life is. Hence the reason I could not find what I was looking for among God's people, in social settings, in the workplace, or in the church. Of this I will say more in the section on 'The Black Church'. I knew now what really matters in life. Hard work, careers, money, easy living, promotions, and even retirement are all good to grasp. But when you cannot grasp them any longer, what else do you have to hold on to? From my knees, I was lifted up by Jesus, the God who held me fully in His grasp.

There are so many people in the world who live out their existence from a very limited mind-set, one which focuses on self and careers. Their journey is disconnected from God. They put God in a little box; they gift wrap Him and tuck him away, only to remember Him at Christmas. Every so often they pull Him out to try Him out not only on their own lives but on the lives of other people's as well. It is the way of the world, the way to keep in line with the traditions of men. According to the Word: "People are seeing, but do not see; they are hearing but do not hear." God is so much bigger than the little boxes we try to contain Him in. God created the universe, need I say anymore. The earth is the Lord's and the fullness thereof. This is a fact! Moreover, He can do exceedingly and abundantly above all you can dream or imagine Him to do for you and for others. I had to look away from people, and take God at His word.

Whenever we put limits on God, we also put limits on ourselves, in connection to our vision of God, and our hearing of God's calling us to purpose in life. Why don't you start having some bigger thoughts of God? Use your imagination to move you from where you are stuck in your life's journey. Spend time with God and God will give you a glimpse of what your future really looks like. You will be surprised by how bright it looks. If you look into your spiritual prism, the Word of God, you would know just how bright your future looks. God would open your eyes, as He did to one of the prophets servants, so that he could see God's army atop the mountain (2 Kings 6:16-17). What a great lesson for all of us who limit God's plans in our life. If you are looking down, why not start looking up. If you are looking back, why not start looking forward. If the way before you is hazy, why not look to Jesus. He is the light.

Another reason we don't get to the place God has for us is because of a lack of faith. We spend a great deal of our time trying to improve the incarnate presence of Christ in us. We just can't seem to accept who God has created us to be that is a royal people of faith. Rather than living by faith, we of a surety live by sight. It is time for the people of God to know that they are not just laborers for men, but servants of God as well. This realization would be the platform upon which our life would find meaning, and our soul would be secure.

MUSTARD SEED FAITH

"For if you have faith as a grain of mustard seed you will say to this mountain 'Move from here to there', and it will move and nothing will be impossible for you" Matthew17: 20 (NKJV).

This is one of life's greatest tensions, our greatest roadblock to moving ahead, the struggle between faith and fortune! We hear sermons about faith in churches all the time, but we cannot seem to wrap our minds around this concept of having faith and what exercising faith requires. What keeps holding us back from fulfilling our God given purpose? What stops us from becoming all we were created to become? What is it that stops us from operating in the anointing that God gave us? Why do we keep missing the mark as people of God? We all have asked these questions or are asking these questions right now! We want to know! What, why, and how to make progress towards our destiny.

The truth is I have not seen too many people truly operating from places of genuine faith. What I have seen is people operating from places of accumulation. They are self-driven to get things (e.g. I phone, flat screen TV, and so on). People operate from places of accumulation rather than places of finding faith, because we have learned that to have things is to have purpose for living. Not so. I have had to re-learn that the pursuit of true purpose in life will require us to operate in faith. Faith as I now see it is my reliance on God alone to walk with me every day. My faith puts the spotlight on what God wills to do with my life to serve Him, rather on what I want for myself, to please myself. For many people this is not only a challenge to 'reason,' but it is also an uprooting of the familiar norms and traditions. As a result, not even in churches do we see a lot of people operating in faith. Isn't this troubling? For all Christ asks is that we have a mustard seed faith.

When God told Abraham to leave his home to travel to a distance land which God showed him, it was a command which required a response of faith. It was a call for a yes or no answer from Abraham, to go or not to go. Abraham would have to either activate faith or dismiss it. Abraham did as God asked of Him. That was faith in action. Later on, while Abraham was still on the journey with God, God again asked Abraham to sacrifice his son Isaac. Abraham obeyed. That was faith in operation. Once we discover faith, faith moves us forward.

Many of us have not truly operated in the faith Jesus Himself had; a faith Jesus not only spoke of, but also demonstrated to us. Jesus knew why he said a grain of mustard seed and not the faith of a pebble or a rock. I think rocks and pebbles are things we can find on the bare ground. But a mustard seed faith is found in a cultivated field, the field that is cultivated by God. Jesus produces that faith, and gives to us.

When you look at your circumstances in life it could be very daunting at times, but God brings Jesus before you so you can take a sneak peep into the future. To see Jesus is to see beyond where you are. Faith is the first step towards Him. But faith is not static. Faith is progressive, it is always going forward. By faith, we begin to move from bending knees to standing on the promises of God. We cannot have faith and remain in a place of oppression, fear, and deprivations. Whatever evil comes to us through the works of men, faith conquers through Christ.

I am not an expert on any of the psychological things that keep us back in achieving a better life. A psychologist is more qualified to answer those questions. However, I do know I personally wrestled with all the questions that any one human being would wrestle with concerning life, purpose, contribution to society and to life itself. I thank God there are answers and there is hope! When the highways of life takes us into areas of uncertainties; all our answers have been given ahead of time and they are all found in God's word, The Bible. Diligently seeking God by faith is the first answer to all our life's questions. I refuse to believe that this all-wise creator would make a mistake by creating anyone of us without a proper link to Himself, our faith! God is the One who created you and He will put you back on your path if you missed it, to fulfilling your God given purpose and destiny. But you must have faith; you must reach for the faith which God has placed deep within the fiber of your being. It was placed there long before the foundation of time.

Everything about life and the end of life was prepared by God from the beginning of time! There was order and purpose in the universe when it was created by God. God also ordained purpose for each person long before they came into being. Purpose was established within you before the beginning of time! As such, you cannot give up on yourself no matter the extent of difficulties you might be facing; God hasn't given up on you, so why should you? Then too, why should you believe that the current situations you are in (e.g. economic deprivation, physical disability or other perceived limitations) are the places where you must remain?

Those who have some power over your material existence wants you to focus on all the negative things that are going around you, hoping that the more you dwell on the negative things, the less you will be able to see all the things God still has in store for you! Those who deny you access to opportunities, as they themselves have gotten, expect you to wallow in self pity. Remember: when all the physical things are taken away from you, there are still you—your soul, your spirit, your mind, your sense of being. That is the part of your essential nature which you must never relinquish. For it gives you the voice to say Nike, a Greek word, meaning victory. For greater is He that is in you than the forces arrayed against you in the world.

Someone once defined madness as doing the same things over and over and expecting a different result. In ordering your life according to the world's systems, the ones which denies you self expression and personal realization of your potentialities, it is tantamount to madness. The truth is: Childcare workers are not mad people for doing that type of work, although some could be driven to madness because of the setting in which they work. Just consider the recent headlines about the White upper class mother who shot her two children in the head, killing them and then going to bed. She intimated that her children were causing her to live in a hell-home, a sprawling mansion as it looks from the outside. Upon her arrest, it was said that she showed no remorse. I could not help feeling sorry about what happened to those children. But I also thought to myself: childcare providers have to work with some of these "difficult children" (something that many of their parents try to avoid by having childcare workers) , I have met parents of children who are dysfunctional to be just as dysfunctional as their own children. The dysfunction of the employers in the system of Childcare work is the metaphor for the type of madness mentioned above. By it and in it, these employers in the system of childcare would want you to keep running without any goals for yourself, and coming to them every day until they no longer need you.

I have discovered that the employers of Childcare provider want to define your existence. It is your soul that they are after, if they are able to define who you are and limit you to what they want you to be for the rest of your life. They would want you to see yourself as their ready-made childcare worker for the rest of your life. By doing so, they would succeed in placing limits on your innate ability to be more, to dream more, to accomplish more, and to soar like Eagles. What an illusion! Moreover, most of them see you as dispensable features of their commodities which they buy and sell, and they hire and fire.

A childcare system as set up by employers will never be able to adequately define who you are. Most employers would want you to believe that the work you do is actually who you are. Once we accept the narrow definition of who we are according to a secular world, we would always end up on the dead end streets of unhappiness and of helplessness. You would find this to be true when you have no job after all the years you have given to the task of childcare. And I dare to also say: many childcare providers are living on dead end streets in the deepest midnight of hopelessness even when they have a job in childcare work.

In order to come out of this hopelessness, you have to believe that God created you with many gifts, that you can always shift direction. I understand the uneasiness we often have in contemplating a new direction for our life. I, however, have come to appreciate the uneasiness. I see the uneasiness as the Spirit's calling me from complacency to who God had created me to be (and where he wants me to go). I have had to believe that the path for my journey was already set. As such, I am on a course of discovery. I am on a journey from one degree of glory to another, even when adversities, trials, and obstacles stand in my way.

You absolutely have to believe that there is a still small voice speaking to you, pointing you to a greater way of self fulfillment. You absolutely have to believe that God did not make a mistake when He created you, because you have a purpose to fulfill in His kingdom. Even if our loved ones do not speak words of encouragement to us, still keep focused on God. What they cannot see, you see. What they do not understand, you know. God is real.

God did not give them the vision, or the plan or the dream for you. God gave it to you! And you must believe that you can achieve what he gave you to do. Start the journey. The longest journey begins with a single step! You must put your foot forward to begin this journey by trusting God. Trust that God will keep His Word. Trust that He will never leave you nor forsake you. Keep this statement always before you: "He, who began a good work in you, will carry it out to completion" (Philippians1:6). What God is doing with you, it cannot be undone by anyone else. Remember: He rewards those who diligently seek him. That is what drives my faith. For I know that God will never disappoint me if I live according to the purpose God has for me. Although we may not receive the reward as we expect it or want it, the truth is God's reward is flowing every day. It comes in unexpected ways. Who better than me can say this after been unemployed for over one year, and having to still pay bills.

OBEDIENCE

Obeying God is just as important as having Faith! Faith and Obedience go hand in hand, they go together. After you have discovered your purpose and the plan God has for your life, you now have to be obedient to His call. You must never doubt that you have been called into purpose by God, in this present time. You are not out of time, you are not before your time, neither are you at the end of your time. If you are reading this book, then you are in time. Everything requires effort. You have come too far in your journey, to give up, don't give up now! You are at the cusp of the break-through to a life of faith. Spend a little more time with God and let him reveal the next step to you. The acceptable response to God is to obey what He tells you to do. It may seem an impossible task and you may even question if this is what God wants you to do! Why not move into a new direction and "taste and see" where God is leading you. This is what He wants you to do. Although you might still be asking the question: what is it that God called me to do? Stay the course by keep on praying, moving ahead, and seeking God's guidance for your purpose to be realized.

As I look back at my own life I know that God has called me to encourage and help others in this journey of life. All the other things I did along the way were just by-products of getting to where he needed me to be. There was a time in my life when I was more comfortable supporting and encouraging others into becoming who God created them to be. But, when it came to me responding to God, as I was encouraging others to do, I would always say: maybe later, not now, maybe later. I had a job, money in the bank, and a good life. This gave me joy, then. But God has a way of getting our attention. When God is ready to move you in a different direction, He will cut off the meager means of supply! God will shut it down! You will not have a choice but to go back to Him and start moving where you ought to go with Him, to where you should have been a long time ago fulfilling your purpose for being.

We all came into this world with certain God-given tasks and challenges. Just as Jesus was called on to be mankind's Savior, God has called every one of us to both follow Jesus and to complete our duties to Him. Whether you are a mother, a father, a brother, a sister, a friend, a lover, a husband, a wife, a poet, artist, teacher, and so on, even to an unskilled worker, we all are called to be servants of God. The difference between Jesus and us is that Jesus came in this world full of faith and obedience toward completing His purpose. But many of us stop short of faith and obedience when the going gets tough.

It is helpful for us to look at Jesus in the Garden of Gethsemane, when he prayed and ask "if God will let this cup pass Him." He understood that there would be times of hardship and distress ahead. Yet Jesus found the faith and courage to say: "but not His will but God's will be done." Jesus gave us the format, the blueprint to staying focused. The will of God is the purpose for our life, that we may have the joy of God more abundantly.

Jesus showed us how to complete the purpose of God in life. He stayed the course. He kept the faith. He lived to be what God wanted Him to be. So then, Jesus is the way, the only way to getting to where we have to go. He is also the source of our faith to have a meaningful life. But we have to continue to keep our eyes on Jesus. As for me, I know I do not have a choice but to look to Him for the way to get to my destiny. He is the way, the only way, the truth and the light! My destiny, my purpose in life is linked to Him and through Him. That is what really matters in my life now.

When we find ourselves in difficult situations, in dry places of unemployment, we too have to pray as Jesus did: "not my will, but Thy will be done in my life." God's promises are still in effect even in times of our distress. He promised to be with us always, even to the end. We should also be reminded that Jesus Christ already overcame the world. We already have the victory through Jesus. Nothing we are currently experiencing is a surprise to God. We should not be surprised by any hardship or trial either. All of our challenges and all the mountains we seem to be facing have already been factored into our journey in this life. The battle is not ours it is the Lord's! God just wants us to pick up our crosses (our hurts, our pains and our humiliations) and follow Him.

When the journey gets to be too much to travel through, we can cry out to God: "Abba, Father." He wants to hear from us! God is always available and ready to listen. I am reminded of David who expressed his own sense of fear, loneliness and the struggles he faced in his own life. God loved and called him into purpose to be king of Israel. Yet, David was not spared from trials and tribulations. He too found himself on the backside of the desert, running for his life from his own father-in-law—Saul (1Samuel:21) and having to take up residence in a cave, the cave of Adullam (22;1a) If God could allow David to have times of hardship, shouldn't we accept ours? Shouldn't we face some kind of trials in our lives? The book of Psalms chronicles David's feelings and emotions during his own trials and tribulations in his life. Perhaps God wanted David to come to the realization that: without God David cannot do anything. When David fully yielded his life to God, David was invincible. His soul was eternally secure. As with David, God will help you complete this journey called life. No setbacks nor set asides, nor set ups, however crushing, can destroy you. God will see you through, if you by faith see God with you through everything you face.

God knows how difficult things can become by living on earth. God Himself was here in and through Jesus, the Son of God. This same God still watches over your soul. I believe it. This knowledge is the well-spring of my peace. The Bible is clear about the promise that through faith and obedience to Him, we have hope and peace to face any hardship. Jesus said: "In this world you would have trials but be of good cheer I have overcome the world."

III

MOVING FORWARD:
A TURNING POINT

There comes a time in life when you have to stop and re-evaluate where you are and where you going. The time had come for me to do just that. I had been in the Childcare profession full-time but walking into God's greater purpose for me only part time. As I started to look back on my own personal journey I realized God has been with me all along, beckoning me onto the path He ordained and orchestrated for me to walk into. My journey to this point was beginning to make sense to me. God is the one who is always in control of every minute and second of our earthly existence. That is why the apostle Paul came to the realization that ". . . in Him we live and move and have our being . . ."

As I continued spending more time with God through His word, I realized my own inner transformation was occurring. No longer was I just thinking about how my life would change, faith gripped me. I began to discern the voice of the Holy Spirit calling me out of my place of comfort and security. I started to really look at the multi-level systems that placed one group above the others. I superimposed visions of my transformation over the journey I was on. I discovered that something was not quite right here. After working for all these years, I seem to be standing still. I knew that I was not in the way God wanted me to be. The place I found myself did not look familiar at all. I should have been in a different place, financially, economically and socially. But most of all my spiritual life was suffering for lack of union with God. Here I was, having done all that was asked of me, and I was not fulfilling my true purpose.

I was told you have to 'pay your dues' to this society to get to where you want to go. I know now that if we follow that assumption, we would step away from God who through Christ already paid the dues for me. I have diligently worked, giving my best to my job as I have always done and yet it never seemed to be enough. I had to ask myself "Is this what I was created for?" "Will God create me to be forever doing this job?" without connecting it to my true purpose? What about all those other skills I had acquired and I enjoyed expressing? Are they no longer applicable? What am I supposed to do with them? Did I not invest in them to improve my human capital on this earth? After all of these questions and more, I had to really pause to look at the cross. It is where I would get the right perspectives for the next phase of my journey.

As we sing in the Black Church: "At the cross, at the cross where I first saw the light, and the burden of my heart rolled away, it was there by faith I received my sight . . . ." That did it. I was not fulfilling my purpose because I was too busy with making the aims in the world to be the aims for my life. I was trying to live this life on my own strength—according to the world standard. That is why I kept failing. The more I tried to run in the way of the world's track and field, I could never stop running, because I could not see nor reach the finish line where the reward is. On the one hand I was happy with a life of temporary gratification; but on the other hand, I was on a path of spiritual misdirection. For the world's economic and social systems either trips you to fall or extend the finish line, to keep you running. I discovered that these two systems operate as bureaucratic powers to render you powerless. And so, I just kept going in this rat race, whether I liked it or not, until the time had fully come from God for my transformation. It was my turning point.

I want to point out three areas where my transformation impacted my new awareness of purpose.

MY INNER TRANSFORMATION— HELPING OTHERS

What is life worth living for if it is not to help others on this journey call life? Is life just about ourselves and all the things we can accumulate? These questions would not go away from my thoughts. Like a mosquito that finds an exposed flesh to dig in to, I was daily feeling the sting of questions in my mind. Before my transformation, I was torn into two-self. One self enjoyed the fashion world. The other self yearned to serve others. Living in this tension, I would be challenged daily to choose between the two. Which one is going to lead me into purpose? It is a thought I kept secret in my heart. And God did not make it easy for me. For, not a day would go by when God did not bring someone who would be conflicted in their life, and would seek from me some kind of advice or help. As I was called on by someone, I would always be ready and able to give sound advice. I place very little restrictions on trying to help others. Where did such uncanny ability, coupled to a life of self giving service come from? I found out in the Bible: our spiritual abilities, the natural gifts we possess come from the Holy Spirit, who was already at work within me. But for a long time, I paid very little attention to that aspect of my life. I was totally engrossed in the worldly systems wherein things are temporal and transient; where the focus of life is selfish ambition and greed. I find that most people have a great appetite for these. They set their mind on them, to fill life's quest for purpose. But they come up short all the time. Because the actual need of humankind is to be at peace or is to reach a place of inner peace, something that only God's indwelling presence can satisfy.

I started to focus more on that spiritual aspect of my life and realized it was where God was calling me to. I responded. God's timing for my transformation was just right. In a not so distant future I would face two forces, rising up from the evil of racism and treachery. These two forces would try to deny me the pursuit of happiness. It would be the spiritual warfare that comes to anyone who is on the path of spiritual transformation. This is where a life with meaning begins. As in Hockey, I would have a faceoff with two different employers, the arena of my spiritual warfare. They both were intent on crushing my hope of developing potentialities and purpose. I would discuss these two forces in the next two chapters, where I address the forces in the form of a letter. As my reader would see, when you receive the transformation God wants for you, nothing can make you fall and stay there. For, the Bible makes it clear: "a righteous person may fall seven times, but seven times he or she shall rise" (Proverbs 24:16).

MY CHANGE IN STATUS—
PERMANENT RESIDENCY

The issue of immigration is a very sensitive subject for individuals who have hopes of making America their home. It is also a mine field issue with very little safe ground for politicians and policy makers. At present, a part from the issues of health care and the federal debt, I think that the issue of immigrants can become a runaway train if brought before lawmakers. Well as an immigrant myself, I know this is one of the most complicated partisan, and misunderstood issue, a dilemma this nation has had to deal with over the course of its history. Only now, this phase of immigration reform is framed by the faces of the new immigrants: Latinos and peoples from African descent. America wants to forget that this nation is a United States of immigrants and, that the statue of liberty still beckons new immigrants to come to its shores. Whereas in the 18ᵗʰ and 19thy centuries, America readily opened its doors to the masses of Europeans, and Jews, today America wants to close its borders to those of a different color and language. It would seem that over the past twenty years or so, America has become a hotbed of contentious debates over immigration, and very hostile to new immigrants. But immigrant labor is still the pool of low paying jobs from which America benefits in more ways than one. Cheap immigrant labor is what America wants but also would want the immigrant to remain invisible.

Fueled by some talk show hosts and a neo-conservatism which takes on different shades, these are the voices of negative propaganda against immigrants. They would advance their rhetoric, and short of declaring that immigrants should be rounded up like cattle and sent back home, as was done in Europe when Africans were sent back to Sierra Leone, when their free labor was disallowed by the ending of slavery. America is keeping the new immigrants on hold.

At one point I too was among the incoming immigrants being kept on hold.

Even then, God was preparing me to find my purpose in being in America. My father eventually filed for me to receive a permanent residency. Unlike some other immigrants, I have paid my taxes from the day I started working in this country. I was told that I would need a social security number and so I filed for one. At no point was I trying to avert paying my taxes. I knew that in order for a society to run efficiently and effectively, the citizens have to pay their taxes and so I did just that. Anyone can pull my files and see that for all the years I have lived here, I have also religiously paid those government taxes.

When I received my permanent residence, one of the key benefits was that it allowed me the freedom to travel outside of the United States. But just before the completion of the process toward residency, my mother passed away, and I was unable to leave these shores. It was the most painful time of my life, more so than childbearing. The immigration attorney informed me that once you leave without completion of the application process, it has to be started all over again. This is just one of the growing pains of immigrants, which oftentimes only the immigrant and God know.

The other benefit of receiving permanent residence was that I would pay less for a credit at Lehman College. Had I applied to go to school without proof of residence (through the green card), the cost would have been astronomical. I had other proofs of residence through all the other bills I paid, my home lease agreement and the taxes that were deducted from my pay every week. Also I have filed income taxes ever since I arrived in this country. In effect I was determined to go through due process, so I could get a legitimate shot at improving my standard of living.

As you can see, so far not a whole lot have changed after I received this green card. I am still paying into a system because I believe it would be there for me when I need to access these benefits. Hence once again, I was surprised when my unemployment benefits were denied based on my employer vicious lies about the circumstances that occurred that last day of my employment in March 2010, as I would discuss in the section on Dear Mr. D.

Many of us look forward to getting this residency card because it is supposed to be a miraculous piece of paper that should transform our lives. I would come to find out this is another means of oppressing immigrants by making them believe that the green card is the ultimate reward. This so polarizes people—those who have the green card and those who don't. Having a green card does not end the injustices of racism. Racism and inequality still persists in America against people of color and continuously against immigrants. So what's the big deal about this green card? It's just a game. It's a tool used to continue to keep wages down for immigrants and to deny people their God given humanity. To keep one group feeling superior to the other, making them feel they are better than immigrants without the green card. The real evil that faces every person of color in America whether you are an immigrant legal or illegal, or whether you are a woman or black is Racism. It is the spiritual warfare of all Black people. This is America's closeted illness, which is never fully realized until you make the commitment to live in this country. This illness breaks out from its closet in the hearts of White America; it comes out far too often to infect society and the world at large.

FACING THE DEVOURER: RACISM

As a Black, female immigrant I encountered racism almost immediately upon my arrival. I remembered going into a department store, and when I was leaving the security guard followed me outside of the store asking me if I had "put down" the dress that I was walking around the store with on my arm. I have a habit which some women also have, that is to pick up an item that I might be interested in and holding it, while I still shopped. I would do this, because I would not yet have made up my mind to purchase the dress. To this day, I walk around a store with items in my hands because past experiences have taught me that, once you put an item down and return later for it, this item would have been taken by someone else.

In one other instance, I saw racism up close and personal. One day, one of my early employers asked me to pick up her fur coat at the mall where it was being cleaned. With ticket in hand and a "white child" in tow, I went to get the coat. Although I had the ticket and the child, the attendant refused to hand over this fur coat to me. The reason given was that it was not their policy to hand over items to anyone but to the owner. This could have been easily rectified had the attendant called my employer, as I suggested she should do. Her response was: "I cannot give it to you." Afterward, I thought why the attendant did not check my identification to verify who I was and where I lived. But she did not. She only focused on a Black woman coming into her store, in a White neighborhood, to claim a fur coat. It was all about race. I suppose that she may also have been curious about the White child I was holding in my arms. I live by this creed: If my own money cannot buy me what I want, I do not want it any other way. I have no need to steal anything even if it is given to me secretly without anyone knowing. God knows!

From my own experiences with racism, from the many pages of books on racism I have read, and from the witness of some of my fellow workers, I would understand that racism is an evil imposition on someone else's humanity. Racism is the work of a race devourer, an individual or systemic devourer. A racist devourer would seek to destroy you, by misrepresenting personhood, and denoting the ugliest characterization of someone who is different than the racist. The full breath of racism would include a systemic destruction of other people's culture and faith traditions. The historical record of racism in America did not end with the abolition of slavery.

A racist person, as I would later find out in this 21st century, would go to great lengths, even to fabricating a ruse, a terror ideology in an attempt to destroy human nature. In my case, racism was the motivating force that led one of my employers lies, to stop me from obtaining unemployment benefits. guess who did the White unemployment agent believe? The readers know the answer. Here then is systemic racism at work.

Today, I am persuaded that racism targets Black men in general, as well as young Black men and Black women immigrants. Racism is a devourer out for the blood of the women, because Black women carry the seed of the promise for the future of Black civilization.

Figuratively speaking, racist people have their guns drawn, their blades raised, with their stones and swords ready to go at Black people. Their racist ideologies are still the same: they are fooling themselves into believing that Whites are superior to Black. The truth is, in the era of the ancient Empires of centuries past, the great Empires of Ghana, Tunisia, Saba, and Ethiopia and Zimbabwe to mention a few, were more prominent than barbaric White Visigoths and Ostrogoths peoples.

IV

BE IMMOVABLE

We all have been called into greatness by God but we have allowed our family, relatives, employers and sometimes friends to steal our true identity and replace it with a false, substandard one. At one point Paul had to ask his followers "when are you all going to eat some solid food?" When were they going to start operating in the anointing of God instead of sitting around complaining and lamenting about their hard times.

Sometimes difficult situations arise in our lives to reposition us into the place God originally planned for us to be. At other times, some circumstances in life happen to cause us to move in a totally new direction. Still, there are some disturbances in life that prepare us to find a perfect peace in God. Since 2010 I have been unemployed and I have received no government assistance, yet I have a near perfect peace.

Truly this was God's appointed time for me to move forward. The more I prayed to God for answers the more God dropped a word in my spirit "What is in your hand Patricia?" I am always amazed at how God operates when

He is ready to bring us out of darkness. God does things in reverse. He will demote and then promote: As the Bible indicates: "God humbles and God exalts!" When you look at any bad situation and it is humbling, the future might seem hopeless. It might appear that the battle is lost. It could also seem that the forces arrayed against you have brought you down to a beggarly existence. Not so. Never! Not when God is with you. God shows up and says Not So Fast to any devourer! He says Wait a Minute Now; I Paid the Price for That One! My child might be down but not out, and this is where God steps in and rescues us from the mouth of the devourer.

The Bible says the devil roams the earth seeking whom he may devour. It is always a battle whenever you are ready to move forward with God's plans for your life. You are bound to face the barriers of Racism. Don't let it devour the purpose and the vision God placed in the fiber of your being. God knew why he implanted it so far down into your being. God knew if he did not embed this purpose deep within and hide it within you until you were ready, the enemy, the devourer is always waiting to come in and steal it. Don't allow that to happen. Don't be another statistic and end up being buried with your gift, rather take the time, energy and persistence required to gently and carefully open the gifts God gave you, and move ahead against any opposition.

There is a saying that the cemetery is the richest place in the world. So many unopened gifts lay buried under the earth. The irony is that these gifts were given by God to be activated in one's lifetime, but the gifts were deactivated in one's lifetime. The dead cannot utilize any of those gifts because they were given to those individuals to be used in the kingdom of God while they were still living. However, those people could not find the fortitude to discover, and trust God to help them develop these gifts for use in his kingdom. Don't be like those people. Trust God to help you move forward into his purpose and calling for your life. Against all odds, rise up, keep going, and activate your gifts. A new reality would call you into your purpose in life.

Come with me as I visit two places where I was employed as a Childcare Provider, taking care of the children in my employers' homes. I chose these two cases so you can come to your own conclusions and ask the question, "What else is going on here, in the world of the employer and the world of the Childcare Provider?" My own personal experiences, have led me to believe that in this modern day post civil rights era, white America still refuses to accept the fact that there are intelligent black Americans just like white Americans who also have a plan for their lives. We too, as blacks and immigrants aspire to make meaningful contributions to this greater society and to our respective community as well. We have a lot to offer. But we have to unite as a people and draw from that wealthy pool of gifts and talents which will make us stronger to go forward in the journey through life.

The collective and individual gifts of Black people to America, their achievements and legacies, give witness that Black people are people of worth. We are God's gift to the world, not to be slaves, but gifted sages. Moreover, the scientific, academic and spiritual hand-prints of the life of Black people in America debunk the notion that blacks are lazy and do not want to work, and they have no ambition as is commonly said. What is really at work here is how White America continues to systematically alienate and deny blacks and immigrants what is due to them. What is even worse is that a system that was set up to help an employee when they are in need will in turn, take side with the White employer over the black employee. This is A classic case of "Restricted Opportunity" from a sociological point of view.

When my reader reads about my two experiences as a Childcare Provider, they would see the viciousness that is in the heart of some of these employers who are, bent on trying to destroy us at any level they can. What are they fearful of, that would warrant such reactions still? I am always reminding myself of this: "For we wrestle not against flesh but against principalities and spiritual wickedness in high places." I have discovered as long as you say yes to these employers even to your own detriment, they are happy. As long as they offer you a payday you cannot have a mind of your own. As long as they think that their job is keeping you alive, you still cannot have desires for a more meaningful life or do better for yourself. The ideal life these employers want for you is a life of dependency on them. For your employers your place is to be at the bottom of the ladder and where you cannot realize your true potential. I tell you that is why Paul warned us to be ready for battle Ephesians 6:13-17

> Therefore put on the full armor of God, that when the day of evil comes, you may be able to stand your ground, and after you have done everything to stand. Stand firm then, with the belt of truth buckled around your waist, with the breastplate of righteousness in place, and with your feet fitted with the readiness that comes from the gospel of peace. In addition to all this, take up the shield of faith, with which you can extinguish all the flaming arrows of the evil one. Take the helmet of salvation and the

sword of the Spirit, which is the word of God.
(NIV)

As people of God we ought to be grateful that He inspired men to write the Bible. God knew there would come a time when His brown and black people will need some encouragement to get over to the place where He wants us to be. God knew that His people would need to hear the truth, know the truth and speak the truth over their lives to get out of Egypt. Pharaoh is alive and well. Anyone who tries to control you is the presence of a biblical Pharaoh. You have to tell him every day that God already delivered you from Egypt and you are not going back there as a slave. If Pharaoh wants to invite you back as a guest, go but be very careful of Pharaohs tricks. A Pharaoh's true objectives are hidden behind the appearance of having good will toward you. Not so! He is still trying to capture a few more slaves. Don't allow your selves to be deceived for a few shinning coins. "All that glitters is not gold."

In the two sections that follow I would share my experiences with two employers. It is presented in the form of a letter. I would address my last employer first because he was a devourer who, secretly along with his wife, had planned to destroy my soul. But God.! And then the reader would gain insight into my former employer who was wrestling with both good and evil within herself. In the end, her good nature was replaced by her White cause to disallow academic opportunity to me.

V

A LETTER TO Mr. D: I WON'T
RELINQUISH MY SOUL

Mr. D: I want to commend you for your academic works. You were awarded a professional degree with which you have landed a good payment job in New York City. It is not to be denied that going to universities and completing graduate studies is the ticket to high earnings in America. Being White is also a password to getting ahead of other races, even when others may be more qualified than you. It is true that being White in America has its privileges, and you have benefitted from it, although you may want to disclaim that truth. However, truth is truth, it cannot be refuted. But let us assume that you never claimed White privilege to get through school and employment, you are trying to claim it now. You have demonstrated to me that you want to be a great White boy with a nasty attitude, born out of a sense of White privilege, a White psychological inheritance.

You, young man, may never comprehend how peoples we meet in life play some role in our development, in our accomplishments, and in the trek to our future. Only an arrogant and self scripted person may assume that their aptitude test and degrees define who they are. Do not bask in that alone. There is a more reliable test which trumps all others for it shines a bright light on our life. It is the test of knowing whether or not our heart is right with God. We all have just one shot at getting our heart right with God, and that is while we are still alive.

I know God sent me to play a minor role in helping you and family during the time you transitioned from New England to New York City. The time I spent working with your family was all a part of my divine purpose. I was there to help you get in touch with your heart, that you would see that you need a heart transplant from racism and White privilege to righteousness and truth.

You tried to take my soul. Had someone done to you what you tried to do to me, ask yourself: "Would you have survived?" I did, Mr. D. I am stronger and full of joy and peace, even wealthier in all aspects of my life. As God sent me to you to help you find purpose in life, devoid of White privilege, God used you to elevate me to a still higher purpose for my life.

Mr. D, I want to invite you to take a sober look at yourself through the following recollections of my days working with you.

It all began one Sunday in March, 2008. I saw an ad on Craig's list. It was posted by your wife, seeking someone to provide childcare for a baby boy on the Upper East Side. When I saw the ad, I immediately wrote across it: "This one is yours." I knew that this was much more than a job; it was a calling from God. It was intertwined with the greater purpose God had for my life. You Mr. D, and all my readers, should already appreciate that God, who is greater than humankind, is the One who guides us everywhere we go. Whenever we connect our life to God, wherever we go God is still leading us to our purpose.

When Christians know that we are following 'God's directive purpose' for our life, when others see us as insignificant, we are still the light of the world. The historical record of those who clung to the 'Vita Apostolica' proves that when others try to take the soul of those who are people of God, even then "all things work together for good for them that love the Lord, who are called according to His purpose" (Romans 8:28). The reader should know that there is nothing anyone can do to you that God has not planned for. When Mr. D, my employer, tried to invoke evil towards me God turned it into something good. Let me return to my letter to Mr. D.

I interviewed for the job. The interview went well, as I expected it. I didn't expect it to go any other way. As a result, the job was offered to me. I am sure that by offering me the job you had discerned my proven record of professionalism. Otherwise you would not have considered me for the job. Then, perhaps you may have felt some sensibilities to my divine purpose as one who is following the way of God. You would soon be blinded from seeing this because of White privilege, the driveway to racism.

As soon as I began working for you, I realized that you were two young people who needed someone with a level of maturity to take care of your first born. Unless you care to deny it, you both lacked parenting skills. I had already raised two children of my own during a twenty two year span. In addition, I had already provided childcare with two other children for thirteen years.

For anyone who is considering working as a childcare provider it is not an easy vocation. A Childcare Provider not just "watches a child until the parent comes home. The task of providing childcare is very intense, going beyond just feeding, holding, cuddling, and changing diapers. It requires an ongoing hourly process of talking to and actively engaging the baby with baby sounds, conversations and gentle touch, to illicit certain types of responses to ascertain if the normal development of the baby is occurring. It is during these times that an alert childcare provider can see whether this child is developing normally or not, and an experienced provider generally identifies any kinds of problems in the early stages of the child's development. By responding to voices by moving and making eye contact and following the caregiver as she or he moves, the provider can discern early signs of hearing or seeing impairment, something many young parents would overlook. The provider becomes the first line of welfare responders

As the child grows and the interactions become more sustained with the provider by reading and playful stimulation, the provider is the child's preschool teacher. Again the provider opens up the world to the child through the encouragement of touching the books, toys and other soft and cuddly stuffed animals. A Professional Caregiver would be able to discern the ongoing normal development of the child.

It is sometimes frustrating to see how the Caregivers are not adequately compensated for giving children in their care a loving start in life. A child's wellbeing is the most important thing in everything the provider does. But parents whose children are receiving care only care about the growth of their child, not the growth pains and the challenges that the provider faces and experiences. The parents want the provider to give all they can give to the child, but they do not want to give the provider a commensurate pay and health insurance benefits.

Mr. D, in all fairness to you guys, you both were always anxious to be with your son and I admired you all for that. On many occasion I personally complemented and encouraged your wife on the way she would always come home to be with "Little Guy."

So let's just go ahead and revisit this whole affair because the way you acted, you left many of my close friends and even a pastor speechless even soliciting an angry response from my son. You would have met a manly response from my son had he been nearby. He responded from the flesh with an email to you. But I Mr. D went to my God to enquire about this whole scenario. What you did not understand Mr. D is that I signed up with God to come to your apartment for two years just like I had signed up with Sarah for thirteen years, but you all did not "get it" or understand it. I was not there for a lifetime of taking care of as many children you intended to have. And I was not there to take care of your family's happiness at the expense of my purpose with God. My purpose in life is greater than providing childcare. So never underestimate who comes into your space, for you might be engaging with angels unawares, people whom God sends to help you in your journey in life.

After I gave your child the best care and after I made arrangements for you, your wife, child and her mother to have a marvelous time vacationing in Tobago and Trinidad, you returned to America with a new attitude. I suppose that in visiting Trinidad, my home and seeing the wonderful place, people, and customs, you could not contain your resentment as my employer. Maybe you came away with the awareness that you try so hard to make money to feel important, me and my people, we trust God for everything, and God always provide. You saw this for yourself in Trinidad.

I noticed a change in both of you after you returned from Trinidad and I knew it was just a matter of time before you would respond in a negative manner. Your past behaviors have been a good indicator for me. And so I went into 'super cool' mode and that you could not handle. You then began to look for any excuse to relieve me of my job. You were smiling with me outwardly but inwardly you were plotting for an occasion to 'take my soul', by way of my livelihood.

You decided to fire me because I was browsing the online employment agency from your computer, and because I misplaced a key. You wanted to show a single Black Woman how powerful you are. While I was unscathed by your decision to discontinue my employment, I was for a brief moment, unnerved the way evil-racism was made manifest in you. Racism is evil, and evil is actualized through racism, all of which breathes within you.

You caused the unemployment agency to deny me a rightful benefit by lying about the reason I was no longer employed with you. Well Labor Department, it was because of racism, and some one's head should roll because of that decision.

You lied in the face of God, when you assured me that you would give me a two week severance pay minus the cost of the key replacement, and you never paid me.

In all of this, your response of making yourself feel powerful was actually a sign of weakness. You would have responded to me differently if I had a male companion who would have confronted your deceit and lack of integrity.

Just imagine what you yourself said to me "Your work—taking care of "Little Guy" and overall work ethics are not the issues, they are some other things. As your conscience would witness against you, the other things you had in mind were the lies fabricated to stop me from receiving unemployment benefits. Let us just go ahead and speak of the other things. Remember the year is 2010 and not 1960, when White people were the judge and jury over the journey of Black people. Let's list the things for which I was charged for and accused of in the year 2010 that was proof beyond a reasonable doubt that I was incompetent and not an exceptional Childcare Provider. The following were the reasons I was fired.

1. For not showing remorse for losing a key
2. For updating my Resume on your computer
3. For giving an alleged false reference and
4. For not being happy enough for Both you and for your wife's pregnancy.

My astute mind has to ask you: Are you for real Mr. D! Did you listen to yourself before coming to me with these charges? What else is going on in your heart Mr. D? Could it be that when you came to my birthday party in the Islands uninvited and yet we still received you, you observed, enjoyed our foods, drinks, and hospitality, you could not believe that we lived so well? You should have thanked God for opening your eyes Mr. D, to see we are not "hand to mouth, a lower species swinging off some tree."

I told you before, Mr. D, God sent me on this little assignment to work in your home and bring His love and grace to your home. Mr. D you failed the test. It will be presented to you again. I am hoping you pass the test the next time, realizing that immigrants who come to your homes, sometimes come from places of having plenty happiness with or without money. Sometimes I wondered: Could it be jealousy after returning from Trinidad that took a hold of you and your wife, prompting you to look for anything to make a case against me. Is this the way you treat travelers who are passing by? Who comes by to help you find true meaning in life? Did you feel good after you lied against me? You probably felt that you got me real good didn't you, that you had hold of my soul? If God created you good where did you go bad? By the way did you remember me saying "What happened in Trinidad stayed in Trinidad?" It is interesting I said that to both you and you wife. Was the Holy Spirit alerting me to something?

You all are good actors. Maybe you need to change careers. Your wife played a good acting role that Friday in March. When you had planned to confront me on updating my resume on your computer she came home and as you all had planned, she had taken the key earlier to supposedly make copies,(of course that was a lie) I gave them to her as your text indicated. I did not even remind her that she was to give me the new set of keys. I was just waiting to see how it all was about to unfold. She acted so well, smiling and offering the last couple slices of bread to me which I refused. Thank God I did. I might have choked on it later on that evening. Who knows what was on it. Mean people do mean things.

Once I realized the true intentions of your heart, I was more than ready to exit. Perhaps God did not want me to stay as long as I had. I would later be reminded what God had said to the Hebrews: "It is time to go. You have stayed in this place too long."

As I told you on the telephone that Sunday when you called me; "Thank God nothing happened to your child in my care." That would have been far more important to me and would have concerned me more than the charges you leveled against me. I also wanted to ask you Mr. D "If I had a husband would you have dared to speak to me the way you did?" Would you have honored your word and paid me? That is why I know you are a weak man, a coward and a pitiable person, preying on a single Black immigrant woman. Did you plan somehow to bring me to my knees? You could not take my soul. God used my experience with you to move me into my purpose. Had I stayed in the employment with you, I would have been functioning far below my gift, potential and purpose.

I am overjoyed to announce a greater verdict that supersedes your lying charges: Innocent of all!! Guilty of none! This is the truth.

1. Let us have a quick review of your lies. Not showing remorse for losing a key. Is that what you planned to fire me for? As a young and inexperienced lawyer your capricious behavior towards me was evident. What did you want me to say at loosing the key "Master D, I am indeed contrite, sorrowful, deeply saddened and truly repentant for losing the key? Did you expect me to plead with you to forgive me? Please Master." Well, how much remorse do you want me to exhibit? Trust me I am still trying to 'get it.' After being Employed by you, I have to give Sarah (my other White employer) a lot of credit. Sarah had her faults, which I will get to, but she would never and I mean never; make an issue over a lost key. To the contrary she would make quite a few copies and leave them there because she knew Keys Get Lost Mr. D, that's what happens to keys They Get Lost. And that is how a reasonable, intelligent and mature person handles a small matter such as a lost key.

Let me explore the other part to this. What do you think I will do with your keys? Give it to someone? Keep it for myself? What am I going to do with your key? (It was just one key.). Mr. D there is nothing and I mean nothing in your apartment that I want or worth coming back for. I love clothes, shoes, jewelry and when I worked with Sarah I bought all those things for myself. Did I tell you Sarah paid me with a good heart? Yes she did! I did a lot with the salary she paid. But when you paid me I always sensed that it was an expense you really could not afford. And to think I was working with you at a lower pay scale. You know I am doing just fine, happy contended unemployed with my Lord, isn't that something?

Concerning the charge against me that I was updating and checking my online employment account, this is the only charge that might have merit to it. Yet people do this all the time, they update their Resume, they watch news on line, they chat on line, some even go on those immoral sites. They just go on line. You would be hard pressed to convince me that you have not checked other employment sites while having an existing job. It is a common practice. However I would admit for the five minutes I was on line, I was not entertaining your son. I did say it was unethical! If I am wrong I say I am wrong. I believe what was really the issue for you is that you wanted to know if I would stay on to take care of your additional breed of children, and I did not give you the response you were hoping for. Maybe you were also unhappy that I used your computer. Why didn't you say it? Instead, you went into a place of evil intent of your heart to bring up false charges to block me from receiving unemployment benefits. And so this behavior is what has troubled so many people who know my background, my work ethics, and the overall professionalism that I bring to the job. Not to mention the kindness and courtesy we all extended to you and your family on your vacation to our home in Trinidad. You know I was planning to stay a little longer working with you, perhaps until the end of that year. Unlike your response, I would have given proper notice prior to leaving.

I prayed for God's blessings upon your family and for the safety of your child. The prayers of a righteous man avail much. That's what my Bible says. I have turned you over to God.

I never had a front row seat to a live show where an actor put on a dramatic crying scene as your wife did. She was sobbing uncontrollably before you and me as we talked about my using the computer, (the only issue you brought up that day), but I saw no tears flowing from her eyes. It was a plot to instigate. Perhaps, a psychiatrist might say normal: normal people do not cry like that, and perhaps a psychotherapist might conclude that sane people do not behave like you did.

Mr. D., my dear I am still standing! It will have to take ten like you and the King of Persia to bring me down. My Bible said "If God is for you, who can be against you." God and I are a majority. Mr. D is a good thing I know who I am in Christ Jesus. Could you imagine if I did not know that this was a set up from God to push me to the next level, and it is a good thing I did not have a brother by my side. Think about your actions Mr. D. They were deliberate, well thought out and downright malicious in successfully having my unemployment benefits denied to me. But you failed in the quest for my soul.

Conclusively I ask again "why is so much hate and evil in your heart?" You were determined to cut off all means of supply to me. It is one thing to renege and not pay me but to go to such lengths to lie to Unemployment just to stop them from giving me the weekly benefits; well that's a whole Different kind of evil. Someone might one day say: You are like the dog that bit the hand that fed it.

The next issue on the list; For giving a false reference. This is an easy one to put in the thrash. All the work experiences I have listed I have done and I stand by them. There are people who I have lost contact with because they have moved and that was exactly what happened. My friend did make the contact for that job for me and then the people moved. I stand by all my jobs, my years of experiences and the many other employers I worked for, some of whom I lost contact with. Everyone who submitted a reference on my behalf for whom I worked, I stand firmly behind them all.

The final issue you mentioned was this: I was not being happy enough for both of you on your wife's second pregnancy. What? Are you for real? Why do I feel you want me 'to scratch when nothing is itching me?" And why should I feel happy to care for another child without proper remuneration? You want me to say "We pregnant?" Come on, you have me repeating myself constantly. Mr. D you are the one who have to get excited and happy, not me I have been there and done that. I have Pat on my mind. What is Pat next move in positioning myself to get to the next level, without a baby to carry around. I know where God wants me to go in this season of my life and it is not to be once again carrying other people's babies around. That was in Sarah's season.

Pleasing my God is about the only thing that stays on my mind! Doing what he called me to do and ensuring that I am doing it with right mind set. These are your children not mine, after working for Sarah for thirteen years and taking care of those children as best I could, I now ask myself was it worth it? I have seen enough babies born in my lifetime.

They are God's gift to us but the reality is they are not ours. The ones who conceive them must be prepared and able to take care of them. I do understand this is new to you; so go ahead! Get excited! Run in Central Park and Harlem! Do you Mr. D! Do you!

You told me you had to take out a loan to send Little Guy to school. Well if that is true, should you all wait a little longer before having another one? I understand it now. You wanted to enroll your son into a school for which you had to pay. You could not afford it and increase my salary for the second child you both were expecting. So I became your sacrificial Lamb. As such you were able to employ someone else (another immigrant), at a much lower pay.

A few more things and then I will end this letter. Are you still working in Harlem helping the underprivileged and less fortunate people in the community? You see why you all cannot be trusted. You wanted to grind me to the ground, but you are in Harlem giving legal advice to poor black people. Why are you really there? Do you want to present a good white image to poor Black Harlemites? To put it on your resume that you did charitable work? I don't get it! Do they know you had a black Caregiver in your home, who did the job she was hired to do but you all had 'other' issues with her that had nothing to do with her job performance? You have much to atone for when God call you to give an account.

One last thing; Do you know how happy I have been over these months without a job? I know you thought I could not survive. I am not surviving; I am thriving and still going strong. God is advancing me in practically all of my plans and activities. I am nearing the end of my academic degree, still on the Dean's list. I am where I am because of God, and not man. I am finding purpose and the joy of living because of God, and not man. What man tries to take from God's people, God would always restore two-fold. Mr. D this journey started a longtime ago and you were just a pit stop on my way to destiny. If there is one thing that you and any other oppressor should know is this: "If God is for you who can be against you?"

You see Mr. D I had to go back to the source again. Like David I had to ask whether to pursue or not to pursue (in seeking a fair hearing . . .) to unveil your deception and lies. But I chose to turn you over to God. This battle really is not mine Mr. D it is the Lord's I just got caught in the middle of two forces that will always be at war with each other to the end of time. The warfare is between the forces of good and evil: the greater evils in the world against God's good. That is why I had to take the high road of recognizing that God will fight my battle so; I forgive you Mr. D for your actions. You were determined to destroy me BUT GOD, is still on the throne.

I end with this; I plan to present my case to a sociologist professor who has made other case studies to buttress my views, particularly about employers like you. I hope my book will be used as a class case study in a course of Sociology.

VI

DEAR SARAH

For the most part, the years I worked for you can best be characterized as "friendly." More often than not, you related to me not as a 'boss,' but on a down to earth level. I enjoyed our conversations. We covered a lot of issues as women and we dealt with every day trivialities that resulted in a good laughter. I even enjoyed watching your interaction with the dog and The playful actions of the cats towards you. At the end of each workday, I would leave knowing that you were satisfied with the work I had done, and I was pleased with the way you treated me. You showed concern about my departing late, so as to arrange door to door car service for me from work to home from time to time. Working for you also afforded me financial security. My earnings were commensurate with my level of service. There was also another unique aspect to being at work for you. You never forgot to give me a birthday and a Christmas gift and I always sought your advice when it came to giving the children their gifts. We stayed clear of religious issues as far as the children were concerned but you also encouraged and respected my own beliefs. This was always demonstrated by your positive response when I needed a day to attend a conference or any matter that pertained to the affairs of the church.

I know you trusted me with the care of the children as you expressed it not only to me but to other friends and relatives. So this reflects the trust, respect, and integrity in the years of our association. It went beyond the boundaries of employer-employee guidelines.

After thirteen years of working for you, I did not expect the way we related to each other would have changed. But it did. Something changed somewhere, whether it was attitudes, assumptions, spousal instigation, I still do not know what caused our relationship to change. Yet the change was evident in that our conversation was not altogether open and frank as before. Specifically, the issue of me going back to school became a negative issue for you. You were not forthcoming at first.

Why it became such a tumultuous issue that I was going back to school could lead to many different answers. Long before applying to college, I had mentioned it to you. One full year had passed, before I came back to you to let you know that I was now ready to submit my application to the college. We had had ample time to talk about the options and possibilities regarding my work and my studies. We had always taken time to talk about other things. But now you kept silent about my mention of going back to college.

My plans were to go back to school two days a week full-time and work with the kids the other three days. I just felt that you would have been happy for me to go back to college. It is a form of promotion for which most people are consumed with joy. I was, but it did not appear that you were. You are near the top of your career, and I have always admired you for that. I have always been happy for you.

So, I did not think that the change in my work schedule would have negatively affected the care of the children. Therefore, I was hurt by your response, when you finally decided to answer me about my proposal for my education. Your demeanor caused me to wonder that you would have preferred for me not to go to college, that I should not have any forward plans for myself. I still cannot comprehend the import of your verbal outburst that day. Sometimes I have flashbacks about it, and I still struggle with it, because that is not the person I always saw you to be.

For the first time in all the years I had worked for you, I would be forced to link my labor in your household to the slave-master creed of ages past. I thought about the slaves during slavery and how helpless they must have felt. Sarah, I actively had to call the Spirit of Kunta Kente to help me understand and withstand the response I was hearing from you. Kente's spirit would be called on in the same way that Roman Catholics call on 'saints,' or as other people call on the wisdom of their patriarchs in times of distress. I was encouraged to know that while in the grip of slavery, Kunta Kente would not be denied his visions of real hopes and dreams. The very same race of people who wanted a better future for themselves and their offspring would want to keep Kente bound to perpetual hopelessness. Therefore, I had to stand in Kente's spirit of hope fully convinced that God created every race of people for a better future.

Although there were slaves throughout the Caribbean, slavery ended in Trinidad before it did in America. And today, we Trinidadians pride ourselves in being a society devoid of racism. We do not have any race of people which limit progression and educational opportunities to a darker race of people. We encourage and give each other a turn to grow and find a meaningful place for themselves in the society. As our country motto says "Where every creed and race find an equal place."

It was in that moment that God removed his grace and stepped aside to see whether or not I will trust Him or trust the paycheck from the job. I could not stay without His grace Sarah. It was a difficult decision but one I had to make. No one can truly survive in certain situations without God's grace. Throughout our days on earth, God allows us to be in situations and circumstances so He can further shape our existence. That is why I now had to pursue God's purpose for my life. The Bible speaks about someone finding a rare treasure and, upon finding it the person goes and sells all that they own to buy this rare gem. That is a vivid representation of me.

I had to pursue my God-given purpose; it is the rear treasure I had found. Destiny kept calling me, if necessary, to go give up all obstacles to the pursuit of my dreams. It was God who had led me to begin working for you. It is this same God who was now calling me to go back to college. As I think about it, God could not have called me to stay in your house and not seek after Him, through whom I know my real purpose in life.

White America does not care to accept that African Americans have great potentials yet untapped. In every segment of civilized society, African Americans have excelled intellectually and politically, not just in sports. Even so, why does White America still want to turn back the clock to a time when African Americans would only see their life through the mirror of self abandoned servitude to Whites? We too have purpose in life and it is not just to take care of kids or to do the menial jobs. The great Frederick Douglass proved that, although he was denied liberty and the pursuit of self improvement, he learned on his own to go after the achievements bound by his purpose in life.

God made me for his good pleasure and not for the fortunes of others. He allowed me to stop by and spend some time with your family on my way to purpose. I was just passing through. The thirteen years were a momentary pit stop. As such, I can truly say, I enjoyed taking care of the girls. The memories would not be easily removed, not for a long time, because it was a huge part in my life journey

My decision to resign was for me the right thing to do. With my resignation, I saw a different side of you.

1. You did not even consider sending me a severance pay. I am quite certain that your employer would have given a severance package to you had you decided to move on.

2. I also remembered when Lolly, the cat jumped in front of me and caused me to fall in your house. I was hurt by the fall. Many of the people you know advised me to consult an attorney about suing you. I chose not to. And even as I came to work in pain during the days after, not once did you enquire about my swollen foot, and to offer me time off to heal or even to get an x-ray to ensure—no broken bones. The following year after that incident, the foot became swollen. After repeated visits to the podiatrist, it was discovered that there was inflammation in my ankle. All the injections Dr. Matthew gave did not help; it was my primary physician Dr. Elliott who gave me a prescription for celebrex that eventually caused both the swelling and the pain to go away. To date that foot still bothers me.

3. You did not even consider that maybe I too might have needed some therapy for the years of unrewarded service, as you said your children needed due to my departure.

4. I had expressed a willingness to continue some form of relationship with the children but you obviously thought otherwise. I did reach out to the older girl on face-book and extending an invitation for us to meet.

5. At no time did you even allow them to send a thank you card for taking care of them. They were always safe under my care. Again thirteen years is a long time of caring for the two girls without any kind of accidents or mishaps.

6. In the end, you did a lot for me and I did a lot for you as well. So that it would have been wonderful to hear from the children from time to time, especially around Christmas, since the birth of Christ signified a new period—one of reconciliation, love, peace and joy. Above all Christ birth signified that we would have access to God and the real purpose for our earthly existence. He came that we would have life and, that we would have life more abundantly.

I mentioned the six points above for two reasons. First, I wanted you to know that you desired an ending to a good thirteen years to be different than what God would have planned for. Second, because other parents and caregivers in the vicinity of your home, who knew the level of my commitment to the care of those children, expressed dismay and disappointment at the manner in which you handled my resignation and departure. You however gave me a glimpse of what other immigrants experienced when they sought employment in times past.

Finally Sarah, when I gave you as a reference I was shocked to know that your response to prospective employers that "It did not end well". What did you mean by that? I had to explain to employers what that statement meant during a few interviews. It would have been better to tell them the truth about what led to my resignation. I wanted to go back to college and we could not come to any reasonable compromise as it related to work schedule. That is how my employment with you ended. There never was any question or dissatisfaction with my work performance. So the, childcare providers seldom are given their due merit for the work they do, despite their best efforts. Or, as I would have to observe in my case, I gave you exceptional efforts.

All that said, I still wish you well in all that you do, and I hope that one day you would still reach out and say: "Well done, Pat, and thank you for the work you did with the girls, and well done in pursuing your educational objectives."

Peace!

VII

COMING OUT OF MY WORLD:
ENTERING THE WORLD OF GOD

Sometime in the summer of 2010, I attended a Black Pastor's Conference and Workshop which was held at the Interfaith Church Riverside Drive on the Westside of Manhattan. One of the featured workshops was on finance. The moderator of the workshop started off by offering us sums of imaginary money. She kept offering different amounts and kept going up on these amounts. The goal of this exercise was for us to claim an amount of money we could settle for to live comfortably in life. Some people settled for small amounts of money early in the game and dropped out of the game. I did not drop out until we were in the millions, because I know I can comfortably handle millions of dollars. In the Next phase of the exercise we had to write down what we would do with that money, and then share those ideas with the class. When I was asked what I would do with the money if I were to receive it right now and what were my plans for spending it, I replied: "I would start a Non-for-Profit Organization. I would use the money to service underprivileged children in my community. I would build a computer center where they can come and learn how to use computers.

My response was based on my observation of the educational system in this country. One group (the White group) is far ahead of children of color, who are at the same age. The underprivileged child is always trailing behind White children. Somehow we as a people who pride ourselves in being one nation under God, a nation of freedom and justice for all, have not been intentional about closing the educational and disparities gap between Blacks and Whites. Consequently, most underprivileged Black children do not have equal opportunities to compete to gain work and money.

Later on in the workshop the moderator asked the following questions "What is keeping you from realizing your financial dream?" "What do you have to do? What kind of personal reflection and commitment are required of you to realize your dream?" This young lady/moderator was asking the group some important and pertinent questions. After all these questions, the moderator went on to speak about operating in the anointing where everything flows easily as compared to operating outside of the anointing and everything is stressful and a chore.

When you are outside of the anointing or the will of God for your life everything is laborious; the Grace of God does not seem to cover what you are doing, because you are in a survival mode rather than in living mode. As the moderator was speaking, I had to take pause and take an earnest look at myself and truly asked the question "What is keeping me back from living the life God has ordained for me?"

I was still operating in a survival mode rather than operating in the anointing of God. As I started doing my own reflections, I was awakened to the understanding that as believers we speak about our faith in God. Yet so many Christians, including myself, only link faith to having things. Our faith in God is for material things. The things we really need God has already given to us. When my attention returned to the workshop, I came back with a new awareness of the significance of faith. It is that we must seek and exercise the faith that equips us to be totally dependent on God. If you can walk out and do it yourself, then you would not see the need to have faith in God. You need to have a greater awareness of your own limitations, an awareness that is bound to challenge your faith. Because faith is the assurance that what God promises, God will bring it to pass.

As I began the tedious and sometimes painful task of looking back on my own life of mediocrity, I could come up with quite a few reasons and excuses for where I found myself. After all those past years of being a Childcare Provider, I was finding very little time of intimate union with God, in essence, I was a part-time lover with Him. The time had now come when I found myself seeking that vision and I stopped doubting God's calling for my life. My starting point of operating in the anointing of God had to come from true worship and intimacy with God.

I saw my life through the experience of Moses. When God called Moses, he had many excuses to give to God. He claimed he could not speak properly and that he stuttered, that he was a murderer, and that the people would not obey him. Moses went on and on naming all his deficiencies. It is soothing to know that God did not ask Moses about his perceived inabilities of himself; God had already predestined Moses for that assignment. God would see him through.

So many people are like the nay-saying Moses. I was too. We give God so many excuses as to why we cannot do what He has called us to do. Although we may not be able to do what God called us to do in our own strength but through the power of the Holy Spirit, who dwells within, we can accomplish all things through Christ. At first Moses did not understand that God was calling him into purpose, just as God is still calling us today, and so many are unaware or disregard it. Do we not believe that whatever God ordained, He will bring it to pass? This is what Moses would discover later on. For Moses was the man chosen to lead His people out of Egypt. With God's help Moses accomplished his assignment from God.

As I have had this time to spend in the presence of God, walking and talking with Him, I realized God allows things to happen for two reasons, may be more. One is: God will be exalted through it all; and the second reason is this: at any point in our life, we can draw near to God to find our true purpose. He is really all we need, in every sense of the word. God will do God's part. He will provide, He will arrange, He will orchestrate and He will do what He says He will do. Once we have faith in God we should not doubt or feel for a moment that God is not in control; He is always and I mean always in control. Our part is to seek Him and consult with Him about our affairs, especially when nothing seems to be going the way **we** had planned it, or had envisioned it to be.

In the parable of the prodigal son, the Bible said in Luke 15:17 "When he came to his senses, he said, 'How many of my father's hired men have food to spare, and here I am starving to death! I will set out and go back to my father and say to him: Father, I have sinned against heaven and against you." Many of us need to look at ourselves through the lenses of the young man's self-discovery in the parable. Acknowledge that we have messed up, turn back to our heavenly father, confess our sins and ask His forgiveness in order to move forward in our lives. The Bible also tells us that God, who is faithful, will forgive us of our sins and cleanse us from all unrighteousness. Forgiveness and reconciliation to God are always available for anyone who believes.

WOULD I FIND PURPOSE IN THE BLACK CHURCH?

When I turned to the Black Church expecting to be guided and supported through my search for purpose, the Church appeared more focused on self maintenance than on upholding members in distress. These are critical times for the Church to show itself to be what Christ intended it to be, the body of believers of the risen Lord. Jesus is getting ready to make His return, and yet it seems to me that far more emphasis is being placed on their churches' theatrical events and entertainment, than on the mandate of ensuring that God's people are in the right position and right standing upon Christ arrival. He is returning to embrace and receive an unblemished church.

In far too many churches, Christians are far more focused on the Church calendar of events. The emphasis is more on the Church's anniversary and the right colors that people must wear. This is foolishness. These practices are not what God had in mind when He created His church. His purpose was salvation to all men through the preaching of the gospel. That is why He called us and predestined us. God did not create the Black Church to fill up a Church's calendar with all kinds of affairs where we Christians congregate to just feel good and get a quick fix. Meanwhile, there is a hurting world out there going to hell. Even in the Church people are hurting because their hurts are not being addressed. People attend church to be delivered from the world not to be re-enslaved in church via events colors schemes, and meaningless celebrations which do not enrich people with faith and Christian purpose. But instead the only enrichment I see taking place in most churches is the enrichment in the pockets of a few.

I have characterized the Church as the hospital for sick souls, yet year after year these souls have been on life support through a watered down gospel teachings. Not many church goers are recovering or getting well spiritually in the Church. Very few people are getting it. For the most part people are just going along with a program of events mandated by unspiritual people. They are literally leading God's people down a wrong path, and no one wants to address the issue that what we are doing in churches is disconnected from biblically sound doctrine or teaching. In effect, we are just another social climber's club in church with a hierarchy in place. With the present structure, most churches are not being effective as they ought to be in leading people to personal transformation and purpose for being.

A Church has to take a very serious look at itself and at its members, constantly evaluating and re-evaluating its role in the lives of the members. Also, a Church always has to be mindful of the member's spiritual progress. When the members have found their place in Christ and the mission of the Church, we will have true revival again. Members will be excited to be a part of the Church of Jesus Christ again, and not feel that when they walk through the doors they are still in the world. As Christ's bride we have to be that, we have to look like His bride. If Christ was to show up today, I am not sure He will categorically differentiate saved Christians from unsaved people. Remember what Christ Himself asked his followers as He spoke about His post resurrection return? He wanted His followers to answer this question: "Would Christ find faith on earth when He returns?"

Apart from the issue of Faith, I no longer hear churches calling people to true repentance. Repentance is a word that we seem to have stopped using in the body of Christ. No one wants to talk about repentance as it relates to a new life. We have brought so much of the ways of the world with us into the Church. I find that churches continue to accommodate things of the world into its sacredness. But 1 John 2:15-16 says: "Do not love the world or anything in the world . . . For all that is in the world . . . is not from the Father but is of the world." Can churches change the world by being like the world? Can we be the light of the world if there is no light in us? The Bible further told us we cannot be a friend of the world and also be a friend of God. This world was given to Satan to rule over and to be part of his dominion until Jesus return.

I am sure Christians know this. Yet we continue to have all these worldly affairs in Churches year after year, glorifying ourselves and not our heavenly Father. We deliberately have to look at how we have been conducting our lives and the affairs of God in the Church, and compare them with the Bible. We have to ask hard and critical questions to determine whether or not the Church is following the way of Jesus or it has adapted to the ways of the world. Many of us will get a reality check. It is time for the Church to revisit its Purpose.

With regards to Christian care and mutual support among churchgoers, it is nearly non-existent except for the few who are spiritually mature. When Christians evaluate their Christian practices, they would admit that Christians must start supporting each other in this life's journey toward the discovery of purpose in God. There is still too much strife, jealousy, envy and pettiness operating in the body of Christ. We have to help each other! There is more than enough room at God's table for us all! Rally around one another to lift each other up into their respective purpose for which God has called them in to. Envying the other person's gift will not help you develop yours.

Sometimes I find it hard to understand the way Christians behave towards one another. By their words and their deeds they subvert and attempt to suppress one another's purpose. This has been one of the issues that have threatened the proper functioning of the Church throughout history. Even in the 1st century Paul questioned their genuine transformation to Christ way. When he observed their unchanging behaviors in the Church he concluded, "I fed you with milk not solid food; for you were not ready for it; and even yet you are not ready, for you are still in the flesh" (1 Corinthians 3:2-3a). Paul went on to say that the evidence of their un-conversion is the jealousy and the strife in the Church among them (1Corinthians 3:36). Just like the early Church, I too have to say: many Christians of today are not living according to the marks of a true conversion governed by the principles of love. When I look around some churches, many are still having and enjoying an "adulterous affair" with the world.

VIII

YOU CAN DEPEND ON GOD

In the hours before I sent my resignation to Sarah, we were quite cordial and engaging with each other as we always did. An employer-employee relationship based on professionalism and mutual respect ruled the day. But when I tendered the resignation, I 'Mary Poppins', became enemy number one. It suited Sarah's good for me to be a purposeless Childcare Provider in her house. But I had already decided to say yes to the Call of God to a new direction in life. It is better for my soul to say yes to God and do what He calls me to do, than to return later to His throne to tell Him I was too scared to follow through on his instructions.

To those who seek a higher calling in life, God said to fear not because He goes before us! (Isaiah 41:10). How can anyone stay in a place of fear after hearing the call and promise of God? He who is for me is bigger than he who is against me.

Moreover when I think on Psalm 8, I am moved by the psalmist as he is expressing his wonder about this God who made man and appointed him to be ruler over the things He created. Listen to the words of a Psalmist

When I look at thy heavens, the work of thy fingers.
"What is man that you are mindful of him?
The son of man that you care for him,"

Saints, friends, and those who are in touch with God through the Bible, isn't this God an awe-inspiring God? God had you on his mind and He gave you dominion over all the things of the earth, the flocks and herds, and the beasts of the field, the birds of the air, and the fish of the sea, all that swim the paths of the seas. What about this you do not understand that God gave Man dominion over all these things? From the days of Adam in the Garden of Eden, God gave dominion to mankind to rule over the things of the world. The Bible says that God made us a little lower than the angels! My reader you ought to know that God loves you and he has a plan and purpose for you in his kingdom. Jesus came to remind us of this purpose and to show us what operating in that purpose looks like.

Remember each person is a unique creation of God! No matter who you are or the place of your origin, or where you are in life, if you have no purpose, find your purpose and pursue it in and with Jesus Christ. It is God who promised to guard your soul. Nothing can do you any harm. For your life is consecrated unto God! No one is like you, nor will there ever be anyone like you. Why don't you go ahead and be the unique person God created you to be? Stop trying to be someone else to be accepted by others or to just live to earn money! It is the most frustrating thing to do. Stop trying to fit into a place, a role, or a purpose someone other than God prepared for you. Do you know what could happen if we all truly believe the word of God and live by it? What an impact Christians will make in this world.

I myself had to stop trying to be everything someone else thought that I should be. I am who I am, fearfully and wonderfully made according to God's word. As I look back over my life, I too tried to structure my life to be someone else; sometimes to keep peace, sometimes to make other people feel better about them-selves or not to rock the boat.

All too often, in the field of childcare work we have to dumb down ourselves, so we can keep our jobs. Is this how God would want us to live and act? If many of the people in Jesus' times had a hard time understanding Him and accepting His commitment to His purpose, do not expect a better relational connection to the people around you. Even the religious people with whom Jesus interacted dismissed Him as an irrelevant outsider. But these attitudes and negative labels which they tried to pin on Him could not deter Him from accomplishing His purpose for being. For instance, when Jesus performed miracles on the Sabbath, people accused Him of stepping out of his place in the society because they wanted to contain Him. So Jesus did step out. He stepped out of their characterization of Him. He chose to be Himself without any fear of what the future would bring.

By reaching a place of knowing and believing that indeed God is the guardian of my soul, I knew I had to step out of every place of containment and contentment. About ten years ago, I met a man of influence, who I went to for some information and assistance and one thing led to another and we began seeing each other. The relationship really started off without God's blessing so needless to say after a number of years of going nowhere purposefully, I had to make a decision to terminate this toxic dysfunctional relationship and step out to a different way of life. There are so many things we have to put under our feet, to be victorious in this life. The Bible tells us "Not to be conformed to this world, but to be transformed by the renewing of our minds." This is a giant step, but it's one that has to be made to move forward towards living in God's purpose. There are so many strongholds in your mind along with accompanying human encounters that would require you to have daily self affirmation of who you are in Christ, and to determine for yourself who He created you to be and to become.

When you know God is interacting with you, calling you to step out from where you are, you must stop and write down the vision. I find that there are two reasons why people do not step out when God calls them to. On the one hand, they choose not to listen to God. On the other hand, they allow doubt to keep them where they are. Doubt plays a major role in dashing our hopes and drive to our purpose in life. Jesus had this to say about doubting Him: "Oh you of little faith". Luke 12: 28b.

Trust God to move you into the place He has called you. There is nothing in this world, seen or unseen, that can put an end to your hopes, once you step out with God. Whatever roadblocks are put in your way, though man would want it to be evil, God would cause it to be good for you. By this I mean God would ensure the arrival to your destination in life. The Bible tells us: "All things", not some but "All things work together for good to them who are called according to his purpose". Romans 8: 28. So going out in faith is the first step I was called by God to do. I would step out not according to the purpose that my former employers, Sarah and Mr. D, had in mind for me. I was completely focused on God's purpose for my life. I would move in a direction with full confidence in the promises of God.

Have you considered how valuable you are in the sight of God? If you have not done so yet, why not think about it today.

A NEW DAY HAD DAWN

During my times of unemployment, and being at home alone with God, I became stronger in my walk with God. I grew wiser in my understanding of who God created me to be. A new day of endless possibilities lit up my new world. I began to experience life with purpose. I have been asked to Chair the Call Committee at the church I attend as we seek to get a pastor. I consider this an anointing! I am the Chairperson of The Caribbean Group, and I am also a Sunday School Teacher, working with the teenagers at the church. Truly, I have not been happier since I migrated to this country. Because, for the first time I know I am working for God's kingdom and there is purpose in what I am doing.

Rather than facing these challenging economic times with doubts and fears, these times could be the catalyst to propel and re-position us into where God really meant for us to be all along. It can be a time of refreshing, a time of discovering whether we are at the places God has called us to be. If we are not there yet, God is still able to get you to the place where He wants you to be.

Now, today, I can sincerely say: God has equipped me to step out every day by faith. In addition, I have been able to steer people into places where God had called them to be, and they have been successful ever since. This brings to mind, that I had a friend who was also a Childcare Provider who as the children became older was forced into daily cleaning her employers house, in order to keep her job. She eventually left that employer. Yet, she kept trying to go back into that area of work, but her ex-boss would always submit her reference with something negative. All of the positions she applied for as a Childcare Provider denied her the employment because of her ex-boss' reference. (This is another way immigrants are further victimized by their ex-bosses). She would call me almost daily spewing her hurts and complaints. Finally, one day I told her to go back to school and become a Baby-Nurse. After several of our conversation by phone wherein I insisted that she should go back to school, she eventually did. A new day had dawn for her. Today, she has accumulated quite a bit of wealth for herself through real estate Investments. From her Baby-Nurse salary she was able to save enough money to begin buying and selling houses.

In another example, (much closer to home), I remember my son coming to stay here with me in America. The inner spirit told me this is not where he belongs. After frustrating himself trying to stay in America, I lovingly, yet forthright revealed to him what God had instructed me to say to him. He needed to return to Trinidad. It is there that God would grant him the desires of his heart. There, he would find his purpose for being. There, he would be prosperous. Today, my son is living a successful and fulfilled life in Trinidad. From these two examples, and many others not mentioned, I was carrying out my true purpose in life. It was truly a new, more satisfying work; I would do in serving God. So that I am now aligning my college degree to the purpose for which I now live.

As I have discovered that God is the guardian of my soul, I pray my reader would too. Set your sight on your purpose and step out in faith. Move forward with God. He is with you, to help you, to guide and protect you, and it is God who would be your best source to realizing your purpose for being.

IX

POOR BY MAN'S DESIGN NOT
BY HUMAN PURPOSE

Someone may ask what your experience has to do with anything. My response is; White America do not consider the skills and experiences of Black people, to be on their level of competency if Blacks are not born in America, and White America processes their education and/or mis-education. If Black Americans are still confronting educational, social and political barriers, the concerns and struggles of Black immigrants are even greater. I have heard some people say: This is the way of America, it is what it is. Take it or leave it.

As it pertains to work experiences, the White immigrant sometimes get preference at access to work even when they do not have the required work experience and work authorization. But the work experiences of Black immigrants are often discounted and devalued.

I want to look at my personal experience alongside an article by Schiller, in which he articulated three causes of poverty and its perception as it relates to the poor. He looked at Flawed Character, Restricted Opportunity and Big Brother.

Although there are countless books, articles, and studies done to explain poverty, and since this is not a book on sociology, I will take a look only at the Flawed Character theory. The Flawed Character theory says, the person bears the responsibilities for their poverty. Each person is poor because of certain characteristic traits. I am poor because I have no ambition, I have poor work ethic and I am not ambitious and industrious. I beg to differ with that theory. Black immigrants face a potential life of poverty in America because racism traps them there. When you come to this country as an immigrant, no one sits you down and give you a lesson in Racism. You are not warned "Beware Racism is Alive and Well", you eventually find that out for yourself. You are required to pay your dues to society to be able to assimilate, to belong, to say you have experienced American culture and lifestyle, so you can go on to the next level. If you can get there before racism buries you in the hoods of poverty, you may find the American dream.

Job seekers apply for jobs in the areas where they have had the required skills and experience. I came to America with enough skills to work competitively. I did not come as a poor beggar. None of the immigrants I know come to America because of abject poverty. Most of them come with the notion that they can experience a quick assimilation, become part of the society contributing to the ongoing development of America, while they achieve some part of the American dream. However when I came I could only seek entrance level jobs available only to immigrants. I came with computer skills; I also had accounting and administrative background and experience. But I did not have a green card and without it an immigrant is denied work that matches their skills.

President Obama along with not a few members of Congress sees the need to address the issue of immigration, particularly allowing undocumented immigrants who have academic skills to remain in the country. One of the rationale for rewriting immigration procedure is that immigrants add to the growth of the economy and if America rejects them, immigrants would return to their countries and create stronger nations with which America would have to compete. So the advocates of this view Would contend that accepting immigrants is not only a forward and progressive step in the further development of America, it also makes America stronger.

As long as America excludes immigrants from places in the workforce for which immigrants are qualified, and as long as racism is unchecked, immigrants will be relegated to the ranks of poverty. Given unrestricted opportunities, immigrants would demonstrate that they have high work ethics, and they are not born to be poor, according to the presuppositions of a Flawed Character views.

Therefore immigrants are not poor because they view themselves as destined to be poor, they are not poor because they have no ambition, they are unsuspectingly marched like cattle into poverty corrals. And the system of racism and white privilege want to keep them there.

Entrance level jobs are dead end jobs for immigrants. I had thought that my entrance level job would be for me a place of transition to where I ought to be in the future. But I would soon discover that, unfortunately, some of us are forced out of necessity to work a long time, too long in transitional job. As I did my best in my place of transition, and seeing the injustice, I knew I had to re-evaluate where do I go from there.

This represents Egypt as a metaphor for a place of oppression, a place of self surrender to humans (or Pharaohs) who deny your humanity and opportunities. It is hoped that you stay in Egypt and get old and not pursue your purpose. I see the plight of many immigrants in light of the experiences and life of the Hebrews who had gone to Egypt to have a better future. Once there, they were corralled and used as a cheap labor force. But God sent a message to them, letting them know they did not have to settle there to keep moving forward by coming out of Egypt. You have to keep pressing on. Egypt is not the place for you! Why stay there and die? When God has a place called Canaan, the Promised Land prepared for you and me to dwell in. I have been to the Promised Land in my mind. There, very few things bother me. There I have peace. There I receive all good things from God. Things money cannot buy, even the things the employers tried to deny me. I know without a shadow of a doubt that God wants us to live an abundant life. The question will still be are you willing to trust God to see you through the journey to this place?

Since the Flawed Character Theory says that I have to take responsibilities for myself and I have to invest in my own set of human capital abilities, I decided to do just that! I was diligent, competent, and committed to working, all of this disproves Americas stereotypes of Black people that says—I am lazy, I am not ambitious and I am not motivated, let's take a look at my record as it applies to employment in this country. I started to work for Sarah earning $325.00 per week and my work hours were 8.00am to 6.00pm. Sometimes I worked quite late until 9 or 10 pm, because it was the time my employer came home. At that time I lived in Staten Island New York. I would leave my home around 6 am and not get back sometimes until 11 pm. After a year working with Sarah I decided to move to the Bronx. After a year Sarah increased my pay from $325.00 per week to $350.00 per week, but now I had to work from 8.00am to 6.30pm. With that increase of time I did not have a choice but to move to somewhere closer to reduce my travel time to and from the job.

Many times I missed the ferry and I had to wait for a later one then take a bus which added another twenty minutes ride to my home. I needed to move. I also had my daughter Janelle living with me now. So I needed to get home as fast as I could to see about her. This is another aspect of this whole experience that does not get factored in. Who watches our children as we watch someone else's? All the more reason I was more disappointed with Sarah's reactions to my desire to go back to college, since she was secure and living well. She is a woman, a mother and therefore she should have some level of empathy as far as affirming my desires to move forward and purse a higher level of education were concerned.

I was not troubled by the long hours as much as I was worried about my daughter's safety. Working was not the issue, Jesus said in the bible "By thy sweat thou shall eat bread". So I know I have to work to earn my keep. I just wanted to be adequately compensated and rewarded for those long hours I was working. I was not complaining because I was grateful to have a job, to be doing something. But there comes a time when you also want to have a choice in what you would like to do for the rest of your working years. That is why we go back to school, so we can enjoy the fruits of our working years.

God has not given up on me, why should I give up on myself. I am ambitious and highly motivated. This is demonstrated by my constant desire to press forward and be excellent in any and all my endeavors. There is still a treasure in this earthen vessel to be opened. Why give the enemy the satisfaction of giving up? Jesus says to be of good cheer He has overcome the world and we can too, if we just keep faith and move forward in life against all odds.

X

I AM HAPPY WHERE I AM NOW

"I Press on toward the goal for the
The prize of the upward call of God
In Christ Jesus" (Philipians3:14)

I am at a wonderful place in my life. I am not trapped within a circle and running around it aimlessly, without finding the door. I found it. To be sure, I found Him, the One who said "I am the door. If anyone comes through me will go in and out and find pasture". John 10: 9

Now it is time for me ask the question: "What have I learned in my journey up until now? Here is a list of things I have learned.

1. Despite the injustices associated with being an immigrant Childcare Provider, there is a better day ahead if we persevere by connecting to God's greater purpose for our lives.

2. When you work as a Childcare Provider, those who employ you want you to give your soul to them.

Your ambitions, your goals, your own journey to self meaning are unimportant to them.

3. Racism blinds employers from acknowledging your humanity, skills, potentials, kindness and uniqueness.
4. A life of purposeful living is a more meaningful life, than all the money in the world.
5. Poverty is a concept and not a state of mind of the immigrants.
6. Every human being is special in the eyes of God.
7. Despite the most egregious circumstances, still trust God.
8. A new journey to ones purpose begins with repentance and faith.
9. Listen to the voice to the inner spirit within.
10. Break away from dysfunctional people and friends

As Black immigrants in America and by being people of God in America challenges will come. We face challenges such as acceptance of who we are, our culture, and our gifts and skills. And there are also challenges to our courage to walk with God.

The bible tells us "For we are not wrestling with flesh and blood-contending only with physical opponents-but against the despotisms, against the powers, against (the master spirits who are) the world rulers of this present darkness, against the spirit forces of wickedness in heavenly (supernatural) sphere. Ephesians: 6:12 Amplified. In the book of Daniel we know there are other spiritual beings in the universe, who do not mean us well. Daniel had prayed and the angel brought the message, "Then he (the angel) said to me, Fear not, Daniel, for from the first day that you set your mind and heart to understand and to humble yourself before your God, your words were heard, and I have come in consequence of your words.

But the prince of the kingdom of Persia withstood me for twenty-one days. But Michael, one of the chief of the celestial princes, came to help me; and I remained there with the kings of Persia." Daniel 10: 12-13 Amplified.

When you are unaware of the forces at work, frustration, helplessness and hopelessness are inevitable, causing you to blame yourself, your situation and even your lack of education for getting ahead in this system. Don't be so harsh on yourself. This has all been choreographed to work against you in the natural but take courage there are solutions and we have been given the weapons with which we can be victorious. Further on in that same chapter in Ephesians, the apostle Paul continues to give us further instructions on how we can defeat the enemy.

13. Therefore put on God's complete armor, that you may be able to resist and stand your ground on the evil day (of danger), and having done all (the crisis demands), to stand (firmly in your place).

14. Stand therefore-hold your ground-having tightened the belt of truth around your loins, and having put on the breastplate of integrity and of moral rectitude and right standing with God.

15. And having shod your feet in preparation (to face the enemy with the firm-footed stability, the promptness and the readiness produced by the good news) of the Gospel of peace. (Isa. 52:7.)

16. Lift up over all the (covering) shield of "saving faith, upon which you can quench all the flaming missiles of the wicked (one).

17. And take the helmet of salvation and the sword the Spirit wields, which is the Word of God.
18. Pray at all times-on every occasion, in every season-in the Spirit, with all (manner of) prayer and entreaty. To that end keep alert and watch with strong purpose and perseverance, interceding in behalf of all the saints (God's consecrated people).

In understanding purpose you must remember God would never create someone or something to be useless; that's the trick of the enemy, to make you feel worthless. God had you on His mind-long before the foundation of time-. Each and every one of God's creation has purpose, the birds of the air, the trees, the animals, and the fish of the sea were all created by God for a purpose and He gave man dominion over all these things. Man has a purpose on earth and his job is to Spend quiet time with God and find out the purpose for which He was created. This world was given to Satan to rule, control and to set up his kingdom here on earth. When you die you leave it all the pleasures and the material things behind. Job said it best naked you come and naked you leave, you can take nothing with you except your spirit which goes back to whence it came. The apostle Paul reminds us we are in this world but not of this world, why would he make such a statement. To be a friend of the world is to be an enemy of God. The world and all its evil, lusts, immorality and sin is just a world of deception.

The real world for Christians is to spread the gospel of Jesus Christ and have a positive impact on changing lives through the ministering of that gospel. When the gospel is preached it has the ability to transform people into becoming who God created them to be. This gospel has the ability to heal this sin sick world and make people find meaning for their lives and their very existence on this earth. So many people are walking around second guessing who they are. Questioning their very existence, wondering whether this is all this life has to offer but that's the trick of the enemy.

Jesus said he came that we may have life and have it more abundantly and you will have more life in anything you do, once you accept Jesus as your Lord and savior and allow the Holy Spirit to be your guide. Again Jesus said "In my Father's house there are many mansions and I go to prepare a place for you. If it were not so I would tell you!" Once again reiterating that this world is not our home and trying to win using the world system will always result in frustration and defeat. You have to exercise your power through Jesus Christ and the Holy Spirit to experience the victory in this world. The victory you receive the world will be unable to take it away, because in the face of adversity you can still smile, you can still be joyful, you can still be at peace you can still be excited about life and be hopeful for a brighter tomorrow.

Our hopes are not placed on things seen but things unseen, we are contended in whatever situation we have found ourselves in, because of who we are. During my valley I have laughed harder, I have cried harder, I have prayed harder, I have witnessed about Jesus even harder and I am more excited and hopeful about the future more so than ever before, because I have come to realization that God is who He says He is and He will do what He says He will do. He truly never leaves us nor forsakes us. We, however, have tried to categorize and out-think and make assumptions based on our limited capacity to comprehend the vastness of who God is, the depth, the breath, the height and even the scope from which our God operates. This God is an intelligent being who created this universe, so what makes us feel or think we can really comprehend His ways and His Modus Operandi (methods of operation), and how He is going to bless us and deliver us from any situation. Again the question is "Is anything too hard for God to do?"

The Bible tells us the truth will set us free. I needed to be free, so I decided to go on this journey with God because my ultimate freedom and who God created me to be was important to me. I had to look at my own ineptness, my own sense of inadequacy and ask God for answers and direction for my life. I was playing down my own abilities and my calling thinking I needed to do that to get a job. I know God had enough of me walking in places of lack when the anointing was right there for me to step over and walk into.

In the collection of poems, "My Life, My World, My Truth," written by attorney Jason A. Grant, he documents his own journey and has come to the realization that one must actively pursue one's life's end, without waiting for the dominant class to offer you their permission. The poem is entitled "The Last Poem." It reads:

> ". . . the last poem should be more than some words on a page; let it be a revolution in a flourish of similes, sprinkled through rebellious stanzas. But this will be the last poem that allocates time for one of my own to say that **we** cannot Do anything without the permission of someone else. Because I am tired of being told about being allowed to be a part of the process . . . . allowed to protest . . . allow to progress . . . allowed to have and fulfill the promise. And with this last poem we will take freedom by poetic bullet and ballot. Thus,

the last poem should be bold and courageous, strong and dangerous. And this poem will not petition or be in competition to be given a token position at the left corner of the "white has to be right" round table. Because the last poem will ask, "if not now, when?" When?! Because it is 2010, and the last poem cannot try to be patient another 400 years to be given freedom . . . to be given rights . . . . to be given privileges . . . to be given power . . . And 40 years after the deaths of Malcolm and Martin, the last poem cannot be afraid to be in power. If not here, then where? Here, on this land built on the sweat, tears, blood and backs of our ancestors dreaming and holding on to long ago memories of freedom. Not why but why not? Because if we must exist here, in this time, at this moment in history, in this world, then why not be liberated enough to have faith in our own greatness and majesty."[1]

I don't know where you are in your lives but I do know God has a plan and a purpose for your life and the time has come to step into your purpose, or at least begin the journey!, regardless of the present obstacles. Every journey begins with God and it will end with God. Don't be afraid

---

[1] Jason A. Grant, The Last Poem (Bloomington, Indiana: AuthorHouse, 2010), p.129.

All Scriptural quotations in this book are taken from The King James Version, New American Standard and the Amplified Version of the Bible.

to go to God and confess that you are making a mess of this precious life He gave you and you need some guidance and direction. I promise you, with God's vision and guidance, your life will be transformed. Challenges will come but don't worry, you already have the victory! Jesus overcame the world on your behalf! Start living on purpose!